What You See Is What You Get

What You See Is What You Get

A Personal History of Personal Computing

Rod Shaw

Shaw, R. J. (2025) *What You See Is What You Get: A Personal History of Personal Computing.* Loughborough, UK.

Copyright © 2025 Rod Shaw

All rights reserved. No part of this book may be reproduced, copied or transmitted in any form or by any electronic or mechanical means, including information storage and retrieval systems, without permission in writing from the author in accordance with the Copyright, Designs and Patents Act, 1988, except by reviewers, who may quote brief passages in a review.

ISBN 978-1-83654-260-5

Printed in the UK

Publisher: Independent Publishing Network
Publication date: January, 2025
Author: Rod Shaw
Email: rod.shaw.art@icloud.com
Distribution: www.rod-shaw.co.uk
Please direct all book orders or enquiries to the author

Printed on paper sourced from sustainable forests

Acknowledgements

There are a number of people I would like to thank for helping me to write and publish this book. Firstly, my wife, for luring me out of my comfort zone to write about the world and not just paint it. Secondly, to my children, who have proved to be a reliable barometer for measuring levels of interest in the subject on a scale ranging from 'not interesting' to 'quite interesting'. I dedicate this book to them.

Thanks also to my wider family and friends who I have regaled with stories about personal computing to test whether or not they were worthy of inclusion and for commenting on and proof-reading the drafts. Finally, I thank the designers, illustrators, webmasters and other colleagues, past and present, with whom I have had the pleasure to work with and who have stoically put up with my pedantic approach to design and illustration.

Contents

Preface	v
School Days	1
The Italian Job	1
Pocket calculators	4
Computer games	5
Microsoft and Apple	8
Art and design at school	9
Cutting and pasting	13
Painting with air	16
Art School and University	20
Foundations	20
A year out	22
University	24
The World of Work	26
Job hunting	26
WEDC	29
My first day	31
My first computer	33
My first files	37
Naming files	38
Back up	41
Loading programs	42
Word processing	44

More about drives	45
Early office printers	46
Computer maintenance	47
Desktop publishing	51
Bromides and the Linotronic	53
A page description language	54
PDF	58
Adobe	60
Buying computers	62
Upgrading	64
Windows 95	66
Text and typography	68
Email and the Internet	**73**
Something really cool	73
Email – then and now	75
The Internet	78
The World Wide Web	83
BOND	86
Search engines	92
Wireless technology	94
Voice recognition	95
Changing Realities	**99**
Mobile phones	99
Social media	103
Virtual and augmented realities	104
E-commerce	106

The Future	108
Artificial Intelligence	108
Advantages of AI	109
Other potential benefits of AI	110
Disadvantages of AI	111
The distant future	115
References	116

Figures

Figure 1. A reconstruction of *Colossus I*	viii
Figure 2. Inside early computers	2
Figure 3. A pocket calculator	4
Figure 4. The slide rule	5
Figure 5. Bin-a-Tony	7
Figure 6. Letraset	10
Figure 7. Adhesives	15
Figure 8. My airbrush	17
Figure 9. Early Apple computers	25
Figure 10. My first computer	36
Figure 11. The Filofax	36
Figure 12. The BBC Mirco	40
Figure 13. External data storage	40
Figure 14. The first WEDC home page	87
Figure 15. Samsung phones	99
Figure 16. AI for images	114

Preface

It wasn't my idea to write this book. I am an artist and a designer, not a writer. The idea came from my wife and my youngest daughter.

Sitting down to tea one day, quite a few years ago now, I was chatting about computing and work. It was something of a monologue, and after I had finished off-loading the story of the latest trials and tribulations of computing of the moment, my daughter, after a long pause, turned to me. "You know, that's actually quite interesting," she said and then continued with her tea. This was praise indeed. My wife, having a passion for heritage in its widest sense, suggested that I should write it all down as I was a witness to a fleeting period in the history of a momentous technological revolution that I ought to record it.

I wasn't convinced at first. There are a surprising number of people who write about the history of computing and I didn't think there was much, if anything, that was left to be said. Except, that is, the story of my own personal journey through computing that determined the course of my working life. So I decided to give it a go.

The first problem was where to begin. After a good deal of pondering, I eventually decided to start at the beginning.

But when *did* it all begin? Some commentators argue that the inventors and makers of looms through weave and weft (you could say noughts and ones) were the first 'programmers', though today it is hard to compare the function of a loom to that of a smartphone.

In the machine age of the nineteenth century, Charles Babbage's proposed mechanical general-purpose 'Analytical Engine' has latterly been reasonably described as a computer[1]. Critically, however, it was Countess Ada Lovelace who was the first to recognise that it had applications beyond pure calculation and published the first algorithm intended to be carried out by such a machine. Could she, therefore, be regarded as the first computer *programmer*?

Fast forward to the twentieth century and Alan Turing (along with others) enters the frame. Popular films suggest that Turing was the sole inventor of the first mechanical device to be called a computer: 'The Bombe'. In fact, The Bombe – having the function of cracking the Enigma code in the Second World War – is usually called the Turing-Welchman Bombe as Gordon Welchman, a colleague of Turing at Bletchley Park, was instrumental in building the first of them. These were based to some extent on the Polish 'Bomba' which was in service prior to the invasion of Poland by the Nazis and the outbreak of war.

Nevertheless, it is Turing, not Welchman nor Turing's tutor Max Newman who is regarded as the 'Father of Computing' and not without reason. In 1936

Turing had published a theoretical paper: *On Computable Numbers with an Application to the Entschiedungs Problem*[2] effectively inventing Computer Science as an academic discipline at the same time. The paper isn't an easy read but it does make significant reference to the requirement of 'computing machines' and importantly a 'universal computing machine' to manage computable numbers. If you need to know more, I reference the paper at the end of the book, but unless you are both a mathematician and a computer scientist of note, be prepared to be baffled.

Turing did indeed design the Bombe in Hut 8 at Bletchley Park which broke the Enigma code even if others were involved in its construction. Purportedly, it shortened the war by two years, so it was no mean feat. Turing also invented the means of storing applications and programs. This crucial development set the trajectory of computer science and technology throughout the remainder of the twentieth century and into the twenty-first. The Turing-Welchman Bombe and other essentially mechanical devices Turing designed were just that: mechanical devices. He called them automatic machines or just 'a-machines'. However, if we are to set the beginning of computing at the point at which the first *electronic* code-breaking computer 'Colossus' entered the fray, then we need to credit T. H. Flowers. Colossus and its successor – aptly if unimaginatively named 'Colossus II' – were the link between Turing's pre-war work and his post-war push to design a universal all-singing, all-dancing machine he called the Automatic Computing Engine (ACE). Running at the astonishing speed of 1 Megahertz, quaint by today's standards, the ACE hit the headlines whilst Colossus I and II were consigned to history, largely due to the enduring secrecy with which everything designed at Bletchley Park was held. The commercial version of ACE was DEUCE and this became the foundation stone of the British computing industry.

Figure 1. A reconstruction of *Colossus I* at the National Museum of Computing at Bletchley Park. The original machine was destroyed after the war.

I ought to note here that this is a British history. Others, particularly the Americans, the Chinese and the Russians were also onto the case. Their roles are described in *The History of Computing: A Very Short*

Introduction[3] in which the author, Doron Swade, tells the story in full whilst examining the 'unspoken assumptions' that now pervade many of the narratives of computing history.

In the end, I decided to side-step these musings even though I have an interest in them all. The beginning for me was when I first understood what a computer actually is. But before I get around to that, I should stress that this book is based almost entirely on bits and pieces of knowledge I seem to have unwittingly absorbed in over thirty-five years of computing, and also from my personal experience. It is not a life story, as the real stuff of life: family, friends, love and the challenges of living, are not written about in any significant detail. That said, along with some descriptions of the story of computing, there are slices of my life story that have been necessary to include to paint the background for a few sections of the account. But that's it. The rest is for another time.

The last book I wrote was read by three people and I was one of them. It was my Master's dissertation. The other two readers were my examiners. As such, I have low expectations of the extent of the readership of this book, but I do dare to hope that it will be read by a few more people. Whether this is the case or not, I have come to realise that what I am trying to do is lay some of the past to rest and wrestle with the present and the future of work. A mid-life crisis book? Well, I'm now well over sixty so I can't really use that as an excuse. But if it is a belated one, then at least it's safer than buying an expensive-looking motorbike and falling off it at high speed.

So the book is based largely on memories. Memory, of course, is a fickle thing. At worst it can falsify the past, at best it scrambles and shuffles it. In my own account of the past, I have tried to verify the truth of some of my recollections through a modest amount of research (mainly wiki-research) but there are, all the same, gaping holes in the story, of that I'm sure. Other commentators would probably write quite different accounts. Mine is wholly centred on my life-long interest in art and design. These pages present just a few vignettes of *my* experience of computing. They are a sketch of how, without me really considering it, computing has become so much a part of my working life, as perhaps it has for you too.

School Days

The Italian Job

It was in the early seventies when I came to understand what a computer is. I was watching *The Italian Job* on the TV.

The plot of *The Italian Job* is well known. The central character, Charlie Croker, has been recently released from prison but is unrepentant. His plan is to seize gold bullion from an armed convoy in Turin, aided by a gang of semi-professional crooks. This was to involve the disruption of traffic in the city, which Croker choreographs to create the right conditions for the heist to take place. The plan calls for Professor Peach (played by Benny Hill) to disrupt the computerized traffic control system by substituting system tapes with fake ones, thus causing traffic congestion and ultimately gridlock.

And so, at the age of about nine, I thought I had got the general idea of what a computer could do and believed that to operate a computer you had to be a professor with an over-active libido and a salacious penchant for larger ladies.

The computer that ran the traffic control system in *The Italian Job* occupied a whole room and so did most early computers. Some you could walk inside. Even so-called 'mini-computers' would occupy several racks of shelving, feeding off punched cards by the truckload. Feeding cards into a computer ran a series of instructions known as a 'program' and that would make the computer work out a calculation in far less time than it would take you to work it out for yourself. This was useful, and was such a technological breakthrough that even *Pick of the Pops* used a computer program to compile and analyse its data for the weekly chart show.

Figure 2. Like *Colossus*, you could walk inside early computers

At this point, the notion of a 'personal' computer existed in the imaginations of only a few venture capitalists and computer enthusiasts who were looking to the future. The latter became known as 'geeks' although 'geek' originally had other meanings. The word dates back at least to Shakespeare as 'geeke' appears in *Cymbeline*. The Bard may even have made the word up, but as is the way with language, it has since morphed its way into modern parlance via a stream of subtle changes, although for some time it simply meant 'gawky'. Current meanings of geek include:

> *'a digital-technology expert or enthusiast (a term of pride as self-reference, but often used disparagingly by others)';*
>
> *'a person who has excessive enthusiasm for and some expertise about a specialized subject or activity';*
>
> *'a peculiar person, especially one who is perceived to be overly intellectual, unfashionable, or socially awkward'; and most surprisingly,*
>
> *'a carnival performer who performs sensationally morbid or disgusting acts, such as biting off the head of a live chicken'.* [4]

I mention this to set the scene. At this time, most people had little experience of using a computer and many, like me, didn't really understand what they could actually do, beyond adding up, taking away and controlling traffic. Whether or not they had a taste for raw meat, geeks were leading the way and it wasn't always easy to follow. Engaging with the fledgling profession of IT was tricky.

Pocket calculators

Whilst we didn't recognize it as such, for most of us the desktop computer arrived in the embryonic form of the pocket calculator. They were known for quite some time as just that: 'pocket calculators', not simply 'calculators'. Their handy size was almost as important as what they could do, an indicator perhaps of our longing in later decades to stowaway phones on our persons. Either way, I thanked my lucky stars that by 1975 I could ditch the slide rule and replace it instead with a calculator.

Figure 3. A pocket calculator from the 1970s, still in use today

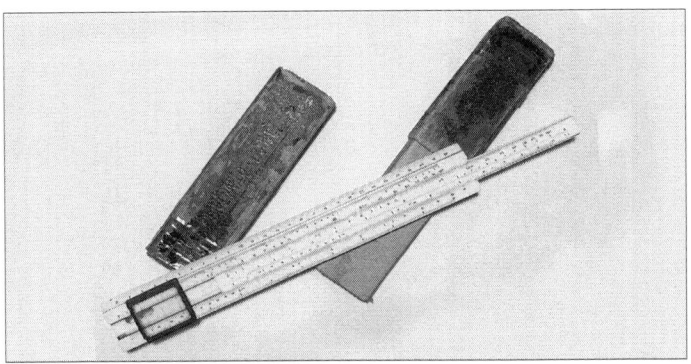

Figure 4. The slide rule

Arguably, the slide rule was a computer too, but it took a while to get it to perform its mathematical functions such as multiplication, division, logarithms and trigonometry. It was a simple mechanical device and was also an effective weapon in the playground.

Calculators, on the other hand, were a joy. Quite apart from the ease of calculation, the pocket calculator had one further distinct advantage over the slide rule. When inverted, it could display words such as SHELLOIL or HELLO using the LED-lit numbers 71077345 and 07734. Other words could be spelt out without even inverting the calculator, and yes, 80085 was one of them. No slide rule could do this.

Computer games

Such a whimsical use of the calculator was, in effect, the advent of the computer game. Before that point, a game meant running around outside with your mates and getting muddy, or something you played inside with cards or counters. On very wet days there was always Subbuteo but it necessarily involved other people. Short of Solitaire and Patience and play for its own sake, the idea that you would play a game on your own was unthinkable. Hence, the first real computer game I came across was designed for two.

Binatone (which my brother and I used to call Bin-a-Tony, for infantile reasons) arrived in 1974 and by 1978 it was the biggest-selling TV game on the market. Binatone is in fact the brand name of the electronics company founded in 1958 by two brothers, the name apparently derived from that of their younger sister 'Bina' although I suspect it could have more to do with 'binary'. It would be nice to think that the brothers also had a younger brother called Tony but 'tone', one supposes, comes from their interest in audio.

Binatone, the company, is still around but my own interest lies with the Binatone game from the seventies. Just looking at the box tells you it's a seventies product because it's brown and orange.

Essentially, Binatone runs from a unit that plugs into a TV and is operated by two rotating dials, one assigned to each player. The screen is either black or puce green and depending on which game you opt for – the range, I think, is football, tennis and squash – a cursor pops up which deflects a square ball towards your opponent. They hit it back. This carries on until one of you scores a goal or a point. With nostalgic excitement, I got it out once to play with the children who, with less excitement, suggested I should try and get something for it on eBay.

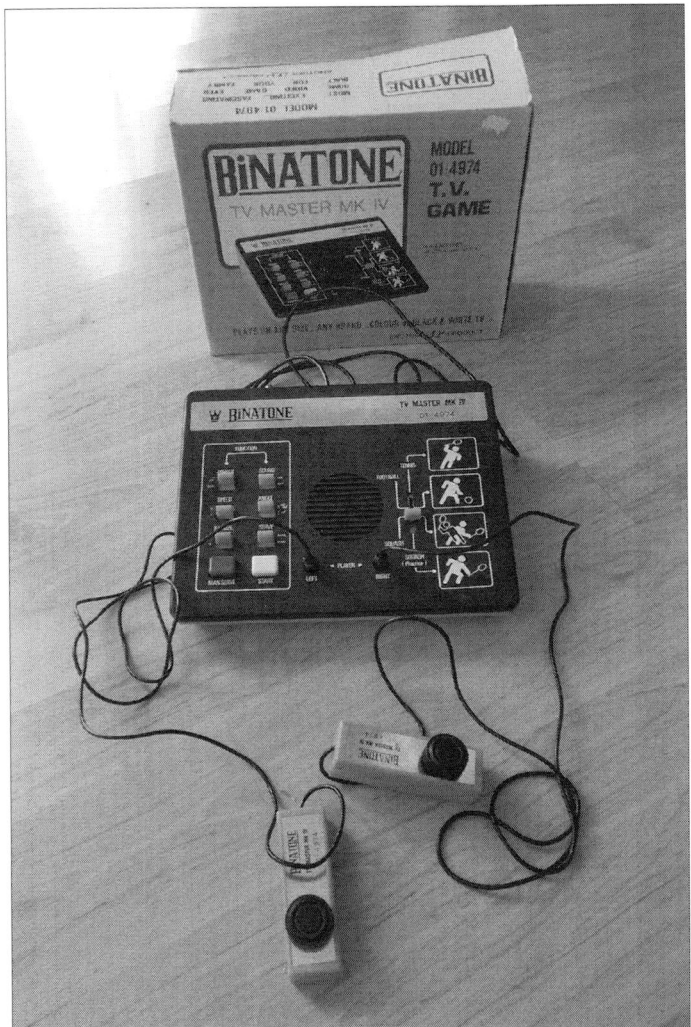

Figure 5. Bin-a-Tony

There were also other games around of this sort, 'The Wall' was one. These dull games masked the extraordinary developments that had made them possible. The use of silicon in the manufacture of microchips was behind it all and this was such an innovation that silicon now pervades our everyday lives. It's hard to imagine that their manufacture was initially a rather hit-and-miss affair, despite the ground-breaking precision engineering that it involved. In 1977, three-quarters of them, according to the BBC's flagship science and engineering programme *Horizon*, were duffs. Checking that they worked cost more and involved more engineers than it took to make them in the first place.

Microsoft and Apple

At around this time, unbeknown to me, and I imagine unbeknown to many, Bill Gates and Paul Allen were setting up Micro-Soft and Steve Jobs, Steve Wozniak and Ronald Payne were setting up Apple. Given that these two companies between them generated a revolution that changed first the Western world and then pretty much most of the rest of the world, it is remarkable just how basic early personal computers were, despite the power of the microchip. Both companies, however, experienced exponential growth as it became evident that personal computing was the new must-have for not only geeks but for the rest of us too. The rivalry and the intense competition between

Micro-Soft (soon spelt without the hyphen) and Apple became the stuff of legend. The competition survives to this day although, as Gates acknowledged in an interview for Radio 4's *Desert Island Discs* in 2016[5], he and Steve Jobs had actually become firm friends, and remained so until the untimely death of Jobs in 2011.

Art and design at school

Throughout the remainder of my school days though, there were still no real signs of the IT revolution that was to come, nor that it would so drastically change the trajectory of the career I was thinking about. That said, there was another BBC production aired in 1982, hosted by Chris Serle (also from *That's Life*), called *The Computer Programme*. The first of the series was called *It's Happening Now*[6] which made clear that not only was the personal computer going to totally reshape the way we worked, it would also have dramatic social implications too – and it had already started to happen. We now know this as 'social media'.

But at school, I had no idea that computers would become so entwined with art and design in the years ahead. So-called mainframe computers were used to run airline schedules but it didn't seem that these were going to get personal any time soon. After all, I was happily producing invitations to school events using 'hot metal' components – i.e. letters that were carved into the ends of lead sections and placed in the compositor of a manual press. With much huffing and puffing, I could print type onto card. Whilst I thought there had to be a better way, this technology of printing using metal rather than wooden components, had been developed by Gutenberg in 1492 and introduced in England by William Caxton in 1496.[7] Nobody, apart from those working at the forefront of new technology, really questioned it.

And yet there *was* an alternative, even for me. It was a relatively new way of arranging type that was quite appealing: 'Letraset'.

Figure 6. Letraset sheets

Letraset comes in sheets of alphanumeric characters that can be transferred onto paper by rubbing, a task that can be strangely satisfying. It can be frustrating too, if characters are ill-formed by the application of too much or too little pressure. They are also difficult to align with any kind of precision. All the same, when I discovered it, Letraset felt like a breakthrough even though the company had been producing transfer sheets since the late 1950s.

As well as being called upon to produce tickets for school events, I was also tasked with making posters and soon realized that I had to get serious about mass production. Of course, the graphic design industry had all kinds of mechanical devices and techniques for producing books, magazines and other print media, but my career was still a distant aspiration so I had to make do with what was around. I needed to produce numerous copies of posters for promoting school events and they had to be produced cheaply.

Enter the 'duplicating machine' of the day: the 'Banda' Although it was a duplicating machine, it certainly wasn't a photocopier. Copiers were beginning to be introduced into office environments, but initially, they could be temperamental and very expensive to lease and run.

The Banda, similar to the Ditto machine in North America and the Roneo in other parts of Europe, was invented as early as 1923 and used for much of the twentieth century by not only schools but also churches, clubs and other small organizations that couldn't afford other costlier printing methods.[8]

The Banda was a spirit duplicator and, to be honest, most of the time it was necessary to call upon the supernatural to get it to work. It used two sheets of paper known as 'spirit masters'. The first sheet was used for creating a design which could include typed text. The second sheet was coated with a coloured layer of wax. The pressure of writing or typing on the first sheet transferred the wax from the second sheet to the reverse of the first, producing a mirror image of the design. This was a sort of printing plate although no ink was to pass over it. It was fastened to a drum and by rotating the drum using a handle, it would roll over an absorbent wick. The wick would dissolve just enough of the wax to make a copy onto another blank sheet.

The Banda was fine in principle but in practice it had major drawbacks. The trouble with it was that the paper 'printing plate' had a limited life. If you were lucky you might get one or two hundred copies out of it but the paper plate would soon degrade. It was okay for handouts or school notices if you didn't mind a few splodges here and there but it wasn't a serious option for a designer bent on quality. I wanted to combine my carefully drawn pen and ink illustrations with wobbly Letraset text and keep the masters for my portfolio, as by now I was having thoughts about applying to art school.

By the time I was in the sixth form, photocopiers had become more reliable and cheaper and eventually they crept into school offices. What was remarkable about the photocopier was the possibility of creating designs by cutting and pasting different elements onto a master sheet that could be retained and not condemned by the printing process, as was the case with the Banda. There were now also many more options other than typed or handwritten text that could be deployed to create a design. Hand-drawn pictures could be used as 'artwork' too. In fact, anything that was black ink on white paper could be copied.

Whilst I marvelled at the photocopier for making the duplication of school posters, and programmes so easy, several schoolmates found quite a different use for what was then still a state-of-the-art piece of office equipment. They used the copier to make buttock imprints with the shameless intention of posting the results in prominent locations about the school – all, of course, without getting caught. I sometimes wonder what became of them, not the prints but my schoolmates. They've probably gone far or else are hell-bent on copying their bum cheeks in 3D and uploading photos of them onto Facebook.

Cutting and pasting

Another development that transformed the low-cost graphic design scene in the 1970s was inspirational. Cutting and pasting was a practical task that involved the collation of items required for a design using a 'pasteboard'. The items were then loosely arranged onto a design sheet ready to be secured in place with an adhesive. It all sounds rather simple but throughout the 1960s and early 1970s, the pasting agent of choice within schools was usually a liquid-based glue called 'Gloy'. A Gloy pot had a spout set at a roughly 45-degree angle allowing it to double up as a spatula for ease of application of the glue that was released through a short slit. Unfortunately for me, the glue would ooze out like puss from an infected wound and would heal in much the same way. On subsequent use, the sharp end of a pair of scissors was required to re-open the slit, but as school scissors were never sharp, the inevitable consequence was that when eventually pierced, glue would escape in a sticky torrent and smother your lap. Hard as I tried, the glue attracted fine particles of dust, which, of course, ended up on the design sheet too. At this point Henkel in Germany launched the 'Pritt Stick', (a glue stick that resembled a lipstick in a twistable casing) marketing it with the catchy if rather irritating jingle 'the non-sticky, sticky stuff'. It sounded too good to be true, but it worked and I have never looked back.

Despite the obvious advantages of the humble Pritt Stick, which I suspect I don't need to describe further, the professional designer's choice of adhesive was 'Cow Gum' – or 'rubber cement' as it is known in America. As a rubber solution, it was easier to use than Gloy. It was made from elastic polymers such as latex, mixed in a solvent such as acetone, hexane, heptane or toluene to keep it fluid enough to be used.[9] It was cleaner too, and it was possible to move a pasted item around for a few seconds before it would set. The non-sticky sticky stuff wouldn't do this. What was also attractive about Cow Gum was that you could make rubber balls with the stuff, as well as satisfying look-a-like bogies. Sadly, Cow Gum has now been renamed 'Studio Gum', not (to my knowledge) that any part of a cow was ever used in the making of the product but perhaps some people thought so. It is now more or less redundant in the graphics industry.

Figure 7. Adhesives

Alternatives to glue were spray adhesives. 'Spray Mount' is the best known. On the can, 3M boasts that it is the 'number one spray adhesive for creative professionals; is easy to use at home or in the office; sticks lightweight materials instantly; allows for initial repositioning before drying to create a secure, long-term bond; is clear, non-staining and doesn't brittle with age; and is ideal for mock-ups, presentations, school projects, and display boards'. Perfect, except that I find that it stings my eyes so I don't use it anymore.

Whatever adhesive was used, there was always the chance that dirty marks would appear on the artwork. There were a couple of options for dealing with this particular problem. Another 3M product 'Clean Art' was a solution that seemed to work like magic. On application, certain types of marks simply evaporated from the page. It didn't deal with everything though so you had to paint over more stubborn marks. For this you needed 'Tipp-Ex'.

Originally described as a correcting fluid, like 'google', 'tippex' soon became a verb in its own right to the extent that even rival brands used the term 'tippexing'. Interestingly, it was an American typist, Bette Claire Graham, a commercial artist who first invented correction fluid in her kitchen in 1951 and named it 'Mistake Out', later re-branded as 'Liquid Paper'.[10]

Painting with air

Again, like google and tippex, 'photoshop' has entered our lexicon as a verb. Nowadays, to edit an image we 'photoshop' it, and sometimes we photoshop something out of it. It's perhaps hard to imagine that before Photoshop, designers used to 'airbrush' things or people they did or didn't like in or out of an image. But an airbrush in the hands of an expert could do much more.

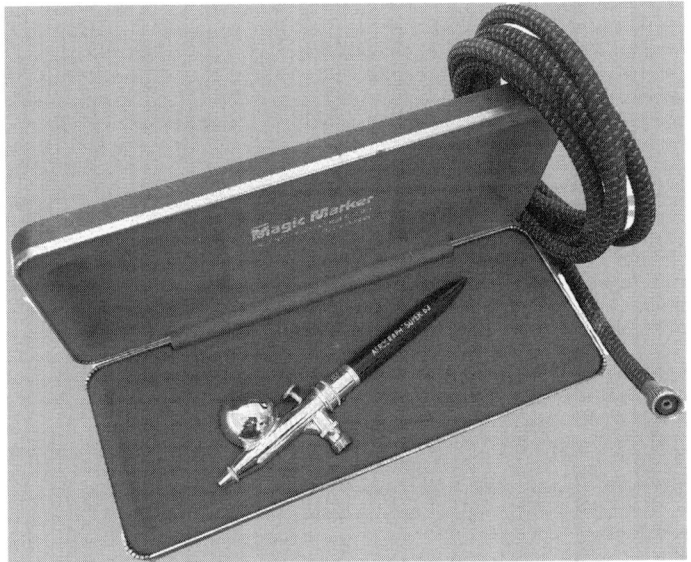

Figure 8. My airbrush: the cord would be attached to a tin of compressed air or to a compressor.

An airbrush is roughly the size of a large fountain pen with a bulbous well situated on its top into which various media such as ink, dye or paint can be added. Compressed air piped from a canister and controlled by a trigger is used to spray the contents of the well as a gradient of colour onto the artwork. My problem was that as a novice, I was rather deft at spraying pretty much everything else in the vicinity and causing a mist more beautiful than a sunrise to spew out and hover in the air until it gently settled on the curtains. All the same, early on in my life-long pursuit of creative fulfilment, I thought the airbrush could be the way forward. I examined the album artwork of the Beatles *Rock 'n' Roll Music* compilation in which the Fab Four are painted with spray. Although I was never a prog rock fan, I also looked to the prog rock album covers for clues as to how I might best master the medium. One was *Tales of Topographic Oceans* by 'Yes'. Album sleeves in those days were genuine works of art and, in some cases, more interesting than the music they wrapped. But then CDs came along and their very compact size spoilt all the fun.

Although, inevitably, my interest in the airbrush waned, not least because airbrush artwork itself waned in the wake of punk and its bold, flat and aggressive designs, I still have it. It serves as a memory of a particular moment in time when creating an artwork required manual dexterity and skill. I could feel nostalgic, but then again, it's so much easier to produce a gradient with Photoshop, and you don't have to tint the curtains in the process.

So the conclusion here is that graphic design at school, whilst it was always a creative task, was also by and large a manual one. What it has to do with computers will soon become evident but first I need to take another detour. In 1980 I enrolled on the Foundation

Course at Loughborough College of Art and Design. Fleet Street was keeping a close eye on technological developments for design and print whilst I set off to change the world with paint.

Art School and University

Foundations

I arrived at art school with grand ambitions for a professional life in art and design, which was now more focused on Fine Art than Graphic Design. The Foundation Course was an eye-opener as I was taught to look at things afresh. Never allowed to get away with a drawing that wasn't 'right', as students we took lines for a walk, drew space not objects and were made to swop over drawings with fellow students for correction. We would spend days on a single drawing, or just thirty seconds. As well as drawing what was in front of us, we were also encouraged to seek out new experiences and represent them in pencil, chalk, charcoal and, if so inclined, in blood too. Initially, I wondered quite why we had to do all this and then it dawned on me that our tutors were products of the sixties and were carrying on as though the decade had never ended. All, that is, except one.

The colour studio was a great place to be, but there was very little structure to the days we spent there. Our tutor would enter casually, describe a bush or a plant he had spotted on the way to work, and it became the theme for the day. Nice work if you can get it. All the same, he was passionate about colour and he talked with passion too. He talked about communication and how expressive art could be, how it could be intellectual, emotional, spiritual. The downside to this was that we didn't exactly get on with doing very much. We were, however, challenged to look to the future, second-guess what it might be like and think about how, as artists, we might shape it.

"Just think about it," he said one day. "We have video now, but that's just the beginning. We teach you to see reality for what it is, but there will be new realities. You will be able to talk to each other with phones and there won't be any wires because vision as well as sound will travel invisibly through space. And you will be able to see each other on video screens as you chat. Technology is the future and it will most likely become your master. We're on the cusp of a new age, a new global revolution that will change the world in ways we can't yet imagine. I can feel it!"

"Yeah, right," we muttered. No one was convinced. Besides, as the year wore on we were faced with more pressing concerns. A place at 'poly' was the main one. Self-revelation and musings about the twenty-first century were at odds with another revolution that was unravelling at a pace. Thatcher had been in power for a couple of years and she and her cabinet were flexing muscle. I decided to take a year out.

A year out

To say I *decided* to take a year out is only partially true. Certainly, the idea appealed to me, but I also failed to secure a place on a degree course at a polytechnic of my choice. In those days, it was a given that if you had something about you, then you could get in pretty much anywhere without too much of a problem. It was a blow to my self-esteem and heralded a period of self-doubt as to whether I actually had anything to offer artistically. This failure seemed to reflect my disappointing A-level grade D in Art the previous year.

So it was time to take a different tack. If I couldn't be good at art then perhaps I could do good in other ways. I moved to London and worked as a Community Service Volunteer for a few months caring for a Jewish man with advanced MS. My accommodation was in a care home for delinquent teenagers. This was an eye-opener of a different kind.

Eventually, I realised that care work was hard work, not least because I also found myself responsible for the welfare of an unruly nine-year-old which wasn't, as far as I could tell, in the job description. I had a lot of respect for the family and the way they faced up to MS but when the contract ran out I decided to turn my hand to other voluntary work instead. But before this, importantly, two visitors sought me out when I was living in London. I wasn't in when they knocked but I ended up marrying one of them anyway.

The rest of the year was split between working mornings in a day centre for the recovering mentally ill in Loughborough and afternoons in the local arts centre – a curious mix. I led art sessions in the day centre and returned to designing posters (by hand) at the arts centre. It was 1981. The IBM was about to be released in August with Microsoft at the helm. Apple had also released the Apple III the year before in an attempt to steal a march on the developing PC market.

Steve Jobs, however, had decided to take Apple in a different and inspired direction convinced that the 'graphical user interface' (or GUI) should feature in all future developments of the 'McIntosh'. He joined forces with Jeff Raskin who was working on the McIntosh named after his favourite apple, the McIntosh Red. Such was the significance of this that nowadays a Google search will reveal far more results for McIntosh, the computer, than the fruit itself.

Either for legal reasons or simply because early users had started to misspell 'McIntosh' it eventually became known as the 'Macintosh', then the 'Apple Mac' and now usually just 'the Mac'. At this time, however, they were working on what was still a prototype whilst I worked on developing a more mature portfolio in a second (this time successful) attempt to enter a degree course at art school. Even so, it was a tough call convincing the interviewers that I had a passion for 'light in the landscape' and that I was serious about painting it.

University

Later in the year, I took flight to the North East and Newcastle University. Two weeks earlier I had asked out on a date one of the friends who had come to visit me in London. The trouble was that Esther was due to head for the South West returning to college in Bath and I was heading in the opposite direction.

The subsequent few years were spent travelling between Newcastle and Bath. It took the best part of a day on the train but felt less listening to eighties' tapes on a Sony Walkman. At some point during one of these journeys (the year I can't recall), I noticed a well-to-do passenger disappearing into the corridor to speak to a brick. What was all this about? As it turned out the brick was, of course, a mobile phone. It was novel, but at 50p a minute, I couldn't see mobile telephony catching on.

Although I mention Apples and PCs, whilst I was at university computing was still reserved for those with a specialist interest in them or who had taken a Combined Studies degree for want of anything better to do. I remember hearing about Fortran and C++, programs that sounded dull to me but weren't to those who used them. Fortran was widely adopted by scientists for writing numerically intensive scripts and had actually been around since the late 1950s. By contrast, C++ was introduced in the late seventies and was a 'general purpose' programming language.

But I avoided computers and their languages as they didn't, at this stage pique, my interest. At this time, it was the typewriter that overprinted mistakes with a paper version of Tipp-ex that *did* pique my interest. My final year dissertation was beautifully typewritten by one of my Dad's secretaries, though by the time I met her to thank her, the typewriter was gone and I found her squinting at a small, beige-coloured box.

Figure 9.
Right: The first Apple McIntosh.
Below: The Apple Lisa (seen here at The National Museum of Computing) was released on January 19, 1983. It is generally considered the first mass-market personal computer operable through a graphical user interface (GUI).

The World of Work

Job hunting

I left Newcastle with a degree in Fine Art and an overdraft. I was faced with a problem. Life as an impoverished artist living and working in a grimy garret (as the stereotype has it) has never appealed to me. I like to keep me and my surroundings relatively clean, I appreciate central heating and, unlike Van Gogh, I am fond of both my ears. What I needed was a job.

With Esther having spent her student days in Bath, our idea was to settle somewhere in the South West. Bath with its rich heritage and culture seemed the obvious place. I rented a room and in due course Esther would move back to Bath from Loughborough where she had found a temporary job as a teacher. We would get married, find a place to call our own and settle down. This, as we shall see, wasn't quite how it worked out but at least it was a plan.

Within a few days of persistent job hunting I was offered work in a picture-framing workshop in Bath that had an association with an art gallery in town. This was a good start. I was employed as Assistant Manager, which sounds grand, but as there were only four members of staff, the manager, two lads, and me it wasn't such a big deal. The lads hadn't heard of the Protestant work ethic, believing instead that you should be paid handsomely just for showing up on the premises more or less on time. This proved a particular challenge, so ways of reducing time spent on other activities such as preparing quotations for customers, I thought, would give me room to manage the staff.

The owner of both the workshop and the gallery considered himself an entrepreneur but he was funded largely by his parents, so this wasn't strictly true. I disliked his fake conviviality and his neurotic tendencies but he did on occasions come up with a good idea. "What we need," he said, "is an Amstrad".

I didn't know at first what an Amstrad was any more than I knew that the name had been scrabbled from 'Alan Michael Sugar Trading'. Amstrad was founded in 1968 by Sugar, then aged 21. After success in the field of consumer electronics and rapid expansion in the early 1980s as a result, Amstrad played a masterstroke and launched a microcomputer that would steal a march on earlier developers of the PC.[11]

After looking through the promotional blurb, it did seem that the Amstrad could be relatively simple to use, so I was intrigued. What, if by entering details of the customer's choice of frame, mount, glass and finishing, the computer could print out an accurate quotation so I wouldn't need to do this by hand? It was a light-bulb moment. I could transform the business.

Unfortunately, the gallery owner rarely opened his wallet, so the idea of purchasing an Amstrad and sending me on a training course came and went. However, the realization that a computer might actually be of some use didn't leave me.

My inevitable foray into the world of computing came with a new job. I moved from Bath and the framing workshop to Loughborough. With the wedding now imminent, I thought I ought to look for work, although the idea of becoming a kept man was an appealing if an untenable one. House prices at the time were soaring and we needed two incomes if we were to stand a chance of owning our own place. Given the situation I couldn't be too fussy about the types of job I applied for so I kept an open mind. I went for a vacant post at the local undertakers and applied for, and was granted, an interview with a double-glazing firm. My CV necessarily required a good deal of tweaking between applications. To my surprise I was hastily offered the position of salesman with Everest and to this day I can't imagine why. My values, politics and temperament were so ill-suited to those I (probably wrongly) assume a salesman to have. I simply couldn't ever see myself carrying an important looking wad of paper tucked under my arm, knocking on door after door in the vain attempt to convince unsuspecting prospective customers why they should install one particular type of glazing over another. More likely, I would ring on doorbells and without pausing, scurry away as fast as a schoolboy prankster. And I was never, ever going to get over-excited about soffits and fascias.

Thankfully, on the same day, I was invited for an interview at the Water, Engineering and Development Centre (WEDC) at Loughborough University, for the post of Editorial Assistant. Drawing skills featured in this job description so I leapt at the opportunity. Frankly, I would have leapt at pretty much anything to avoid digging graves or selling panes of glass to strangers.

WEDC

Based in the Department of Civil Engineering, the centre was (and still is) known by its acronym WEDC, pronounced 'wed-eck'. What appealed to me about this job was not only the possibility of using my drawing skills with which to earn a living but in so doing I would be supporting the centre's mission of doing good things in water and sanitation in developing countries. Water and sanitation as an academic discipline, I knew little about, but as a student at Newcastle University I had been treasurer of Third World First, a club that also had the general aim of doing good in poor countries, albeit with less focus. I'm not sure what, if any good we did, but we did make lots of banners. This was the time of the Ethiopian famine and of Bob Geldolf, Midge Ure and Band Aid trying and succeeding to do something about it. For my part, I joined the Band Aid bandwagon and went on marches.

I wanted the job at WEDC for a number of reasons. Boasting a degree in Fine Art and a lofty interest in international development I thought I might be in with a chance. Before the interview, I asked the leader of the group if he would like me to bring along a portfolio of my artwork for inspection. To my astonishment, he only wanted me to bring along drawings I'd done of people sitting on the toilet.

So taken aback was I, that I wondered whether, in fact, this really was the job for me. But I was curious. Needless to say, my portfolio at the time was missing the vital collection of illustrations that could sway the appointment in my favour. Still uncertain as to whether this was a sky-hook type of joke or not, I hurriedly produced a few sketches and set off to attend the formal interview.

The interview went well, not least because I was made to feel at ease by all three interviewers who took it in turns to have a one-to-one chat about the post. One of the interviewers (who later became my line manager, mentor and ultimately friend) asked me how I felt about setting up a desktop publishing system. "A desktop what?" I was thinking, just managing to say with confidence that I would very much like to.

I got the job and so started my love/hate relationship with computers. Looking back I rather wished I had discovered mindfulness before it became a popular pastime for the middle classes. But I was young and hungry to learn and I wasn't prepared to stop and be obsessively curious about my breath.

So the scene in which this fiery relationship with the machine is played out, is a small academic unit within an engineering department of a higher educational institution. Personal computing at a university by now was awash with possibilities. And for me, graphics were back.

My first day

On my first day I was made to feel very welcome and if there was anything I wanted I should just ask. I asked if I could take a holiday, which I took three weeks later. But look, it had been a busy time. I had moved to Loughborough, found a job, was to be married and about to move into a new home so it was only right that I took some time off for a honeymoon. Unknowingly, I had become an early advocate of what is now known as 'work-life balance'.

Ironically, as I waited for a computer to arrive, I had to use Letraset for my first task – that is after tidying up a dusty room and clearing out a filing cabinet. I was to design a decision chart that would enable anyone who had the intention of building their own toilet in a developing country to choose the right sort, given a certain number of pre-conditions. It sounded easy, but we are not talking here about a choice between white or coloured ceramics, but about a choice between simple pit latrines; pour-flush latrines; twin-pit latrines; ventilated improved pit latrines; twin pit ventilated latrines; compost latrines; aqua privies; cess pits; septic tanks and others. This was going to be a challenge.

As well as Letraset, I dug out my ink pens and started to work something out in draft. Not only were there a large number of pre-conditions, other factors were equally as numerous too. These included the preferred method of anal cleansing; how much (if any) water was available for flushing; affordability; whether there is a high demand for faecal waste (surely not); how much land is available; groundwater levels; and above all, whether a community actually wants a toilet at all. Defecating in the open, as hazardous as it is for human health, can be less smelly than a poorly maintained loo and it doesn't require ventilation.

The chart was going to be my first professional piece of work and was eventually published in a journal called *Waterlines*. In the meantime, I had worked on other 'technical briefs' laying type and illustrations onto pasting sheets 30% larger than the final printed page to maximize the quality of the print. It felt like a real job. These sheets featured pale blue guides so that items could be aligned against pre-determined margins. It was a matter of cut and paste using real scissors and Cow Gum. I used Tipp-ex and Clean Art to cover or remove smudges.

My first computer

I had been promised a computer on the day I arrived but I wasn't sure at first which computer I was going to get. During the early 1980s, the BBC started what became known as the *BBC Computer Literacy Project*[12] which was a response to the increasing number of predictions of the impact and effect that computers would have on the economy, industry and lifestyle of the UK. The BBC wanted to profile a new machine in *The Computer Programme*. To this end, in association with Acorn, the BBC developed a computer – the 'BBC Micro' dubbed 'the Beeb' by users. The point was that the Beeb should be able to perform a range of tasks from programming and displaying graphics to playing sounds and music. Acorn won the contract despite stiff competition as it was already working on a prototype that exceeded the BBC's specifications. Various models ensued which on release became popular in educational institutions including, as it happens, WEDC.

The other possibility was the Amstrad 1512 personal computer (PC) which I didn't get my hands on in Bath. Better still though, was the newer and 'faster' Amstrad 1640. Although they were by no means the first machines Amstrad had designed, they became hugely popular capturing 25% of the European market, and what's more, they had teamed up with Microsoft.[13] I remember that about this time my Dad brought one home from work. He opened the box, took one look at it, scratched his head and promptly shut the lid. He never touched a computer again. There's a part of me that envies that.

Eventually, the Amstrad 1640 arrived with a note telling me that DOS had been 'installed'. It's hard to think back now but to have something installed used to be a physical activity. Somebody would come along at home and install a wardrobe, or a kitchen appliance maybe. I knew what 'dossing' was, having perfected the art at university, but DOS, as it turned out, was different. It was a noun. It was an *operating system.*

The D of DOS was short for 'disk' and was usually preceded by MS for Microsoft. So MS-DOS meant Microsoft Disk Operating System. This was the first piece of jargon I came across but it was just the start.

It became abundantly clear from the outset that I was going to have to resign myself to learning what I labelled 'geek speak' hence the reference to geeks earlier. The most remarkable piece of geek speak I came across in the early days was 'WYSIWYG', pronounced 'whizzy-wig'. WYSIWYG is, in fact, an acronym for 'what you see is what you get' and describes the relationship between what appeared on a computer monitor and what actually emerged from a printer. Why you would ever want to get what you *didn't* see on your screen was something of a mystery to me so when the industry got over-excited about whizzy-wig, I didn't. Surely, it was obvious that we, the humble users, would want to see in print what actually appeared on the screen. Imagine if the Pope had asked Leonardo da Vinci to paint the Madonna with Child but he rocked up with the Mona Lisa. The Mona Lisa is a fine painting but it wouldn't have been what he wanted. But I get ahead of myself. I have yet to switch the computer on.

Switching on the computer meant booting it. This is a term I still find curious. Why the IT industry had to dream up a new term for switching a computer on when 'switching on' seemed to be reasonably apt, I've no idea. One can only imagine that it was born out of frustration similar to that of Basil Fawlty attempting to re-start an Austin 1300. I have had to boot every computer I have used for many years now and have rebooted them time and time again when booting them once didn't work. I have applied both hard boots and soft boots depending on how severe the problems were.

Within a day of the arrival of the Amstrad, I had found how to boot it without applying pressure from one or other of my feet and watched the electronic beast splutter into life. Within two days I had created some 'files' and came to the realization that I would need to get to grips with organizing the dozen or so I had into some kind of order. It was obvious that I was more than likely going to create quite a few more files in due course so some kind of system was called for and the sooner the better.

Figure 10. My first computer, an Amstrad 1640 in my first office. Note the dot matrix printer on the left and the Cow Gum and Tipp-ex on the right, still essential items for the office in 1988.

Figure 11.
Before personal computers there was the Filofax. The name originates from an abbreviation of the phrase "file of facts". The name was first coined when the UK company was founded in 1921.

Popularity grew enormously during the early 1980s due to its association with Yuppie culture, where it was regarded as a 'must-have' accessory in the days before electronic organizers.

My first files

It eventually occurred to me that the physical filing cabinet I had so dutifully cleaned out on my first day was no longer going to be the principal way of managing files. It was possible to do this on the computer using 'directories' and this was all very pleasing. Having created a few directories I thought the filing was done and dusted. However, dust is never done, it just keeps coming back. Whosoever coined the phrase 'done and dusted' had plainly never brushed a finger across a mantelpiece and thought how odd it was that layers of grime that had recently been wiped away could reappear within hours. Likewise my structure of directories (later known as folders) needed constant attention as it does to this day.

By now I knew that the files and directories resided on the hard disk of my computer. The fact that it was called a hard disk and not just a disk led me to believe that there must be other kind of disks and indeed, of course, there were. Soft disks, perhaps? Well, not exactly. They were floppy. I am no computer engineer but even I could see that a disk that was floppy was a disk asking for trouble. It was also clear that at times it would be necessary to pass a file from one computer to another and that there had to be a means of doing this. With a floppy disk in my hand, I now came across another new term: 'drive'. And a hard disk wasn't just called a hard disk, oh no. It was also a hard drive.

The floppy disk, however, wasn't a drive but it fitted into a drive: the floppy drive. So by copying a file from the hard disk to what became known simply as one's floppy meant that it could be inserted into a colleague's drive and data would be exchanged. It's difficult to describe this without it sounding rude.

Even though they carried far more data than their predecessors, the cassettes, the problem with the early floppy disks is that they were just that: floppy. If you accidentally placed a hot mug of coffee on one believing it to be a coaster, then that would be the end of it. Even at the best of times they would churn away and grunt. Copying done, they would pop out of the drive wondering what all the fuss was about. At five and a quarter inches they were a good size. What was needed though was another kind of floppy disk, which, yes, was also hard. So eventually along came the three and a half inch floppy disk which was altogether very much more satisfactory.

Naming files

One of the curiosities of early computer files, whether they were stored on a hard disk or on a floppy, was that it took a good deal of imagination to name them. The problem with naming files or directories back in the day was that they could only be described using a maximum of eight characters. Now this is OK for a leaflet because you can call the file 'leaflet' and have a character to spare. If you had up to nine leaflets then you were still OK as you could use 'leaflet1', 'leaflet2', 'leaflet3', etc. However, if (as I did) you had to extend your collection of leaflets to 10 you began to get into trouble. Leaflet 10 became 'leafle10'.

Next came the challenge of describing the contents of the leaflets. Leaflet 10 about water became 'leawat10'. Fast-forward a few months and someone asks you to revise that leaflet about water (of which there may initially have been a number of revisions as it passed from editor to editor so had been renamed 'lewat10d'), then you can begin to see the problem.

Lewat10d was hiding amongst a list of other now meaningless file names including 'pwsscse8' which referred to the 1988 short course in *Practical Water Supply and Sanitation (PWSS)*. What else could I do? The file extensions could only be used to describe the nature of the file – whether it was, say, a text file (txt) or a document (the familiar doc, now docx) or then, the not so familiar 'tagged image format file' (tiff).

I very quickly began to speak like a geek. Coupled with the tendency to apply acronyms to course titles including the delightfully apt 'wee wee' for the MSc course in *Water and Waste Engineering (WWE)* and the necessity of describing the status of a particular task, to my dismay, I found I was uttering sentences along the lines of: "I've just got to import the text and tiff files to the wee wee doc and save it to the floppy." This was all very distressing.

Figure 12. The BBC Micro, dubbed 'The Beeb' at the National Museum of Computing at Bletchley Park.

Figure 13. *Top left:* 5.25" floppy disk. *Top right:* 3.5" floppy disk *Below left:* CD for data storage. *Below right:* Large amounts of data can be stored on USB 'sticks' and other external drives.

Back up

Floppy disks weren't just used for transferring files from one computer to another, however. They were also 'back-up'. Like so many computing terms I had only come across back-up in a quite different context. To back up was to reverse a car into a drive, and a drive, as we have seen, is another computer term and not just a slab of tarmac on which you parked a car.

To back-up now was to make sure you had copies of your files should anything go wrong with your original ones. But why *should* anything go wrong? Computing was, after all, just about noughts and ones wasn't it? Arguably, according to one theory, Stonehenge is a computer, as it is said that it calculated the best time of year to grow crops. As far as we know, this didn't go wrong. Computer files today are in the end just 'packets of data' stored in units called bytes (a byte being the lowest unit of digital information made up of eight bits). Although I don't want to speak ill of the newly released genie out of the bottle we now call IT, all this stuff about bytes really isn't rocket science.

So I was initially sceptical about the need to backup but I soon became a believer, even though in the early days it induced an uncomfortable level of paranoia. This was because I had enquired about the possible problems that owning and using a computer might cause. I was told that above all my computer might crash. I was mystified. I took a look at the Amstrad, which stood as sturdily as Stonehenge on my desk, and it didn't move. It wasn't going to move. There was no object in sight that looked liked it might collide with it. "Get away, you cannot be serious!" I protested to a colleague, mirroring the objection of John McKenroe when he lost a point playing tennis.

Nowadays we know what a computer crash means and admittedly storing weeks of work on a new machine that might do so without a way of retrieving the work one might 'lose' did seem foolhardy. All the same, backing-up added another dimension to the world of work and with it came the evangelical assumption that everything has to be saved.

So managing computer files was a challenge, but along with files, we also needed to get to grips with programs and they needed to be loaded. This sounded dangerous, but it just meant a way of transferring them to a computer.

Loading programs

In the mid 80s, programs came on floppy disks as it was more or less the only way of loading them. (For over thirty-five years now I have been slightly irritated by the necessity of spelling 'programs' the American way, as it irritates me too that I have to spell disc, 'disk'. But at least – in the UK anyhow – it helps us to know that we are talking computing.)

Initially a word processing program, for example, would happily fit onto a single disk. The rapid advancement of programs, however, wasn't matched by the development of the floppy disk. At one point, as I loaded the latest and final version of the page layout software 'PageMaker', I was up to a dozen or so floppy disks, each stuttering and moaning on installation. But then came CDs. Music CDs may have spoilt the fun of the album artist but they were a godsend when they eventually became a means of storing other forms of data including programs, at least for a while anyway.

A program, I soon discovered, is just a sequence of instructions for the computer. Programs usually have an 'executable' file, one that the computer can use to perform the instructions. These instructions are written in machine code, which only the computer can read, but there is also 'source code' which allows a programmer to write the instructions in the first place. Clever.

The source code is usually text, but with a difference. Though code is not a central concern of this story (as I don't know much about it) some of the conventions used to write source code, the preserve of the programmer, also spilled over into the conventions that were used to write a letter using an early word processor. To write a letter nowadays we would open a new file and start writing. In the 80s it wasn't so simple if you wanted to dispense with your fountain pen. Before the computer age, words were either spoken, listened to, written down or read. Now, however, they are 'processed' too.

Word processing

Probably, out of all the software at our fingertips, word processing programs are the most ubiquitous. On just about every personal computer you will find a word processing program, certainly on computers for offices. It was eventually Microsoft that captured the market for such programs with *Word,* but in the early days there were a number of alternatives.

The first word processing program I used was *Tasword.* It was basic and initially that suited me fine. I could type and if I got it wrong I could replace typos without resorting to Tipp-Ex. This was great.

Quickly, I also saw the benefit of using a range of font styles such as bold, italic, aligned text and perhaps bullet points too, so I flipped through the manual to see if I could do this. Yes, I could but I had to use code. Nowadays, of course, all we need to do is highlight a passage of text, click on an icon and bingo – the text is set to a format of our choosing. Before the introduction of the 'graphical user interface' (GUI) all I had, and indeed everyone had to play with, was the alphabet and numbers – or more specifically 'ASCII' text, a 7-bit character set containing 128 characters; the numbers from 0-9, the upper and lower case English letters from A to Z, and some special characters. It seemed unnecessarily complicated but undeterred, I had a go.

Now consider the following sentence, composed with a few basic styles:

The quick **brown** fox *jumps* <u>over</u> the lazy ***dog***.

Not too demanding you might think, but the means of rendering this sentence using an early word processor would be thus:

    \<p>\<center>The quick \brown \fox \<ital>jumps \</ital>\<ul>over\</ul> the lazy \\<ital>dog\</ital>\\</center>\</p>

So not very neat, but it was possible. It sufficed for the odd sentence here or there but for longer passages of text you had to keep your wits about you. If you failed to close the italic type, say, by omitting the forward slash in \</ital>, then the remainder of your entire document would render in italic. This wasn't ideal, but at the time it was all there was.

More about drives

It's worth mentioning by way of an aside that MS-DOS assigned alphabetical identifiers to drives. 'A' was the floppy drive and 'C' was the hard drive. 'B' was used for labelling a secondary floppy drive if you were lucky enough to own a computer that had one. The Amstrad was configured to load MS-DOS when it was switched on and so a black screen with the characters C:\> flickered into place. (It had 'booted to C'.) This was known as the command line. 'C' meant that the hard drive was primed for action. I opened *Tasword* to create my first file which contained my name and not much else.

Early office printers

The Amstrad with all its idiosyncrasies was undoubtedly a step forward in the world of everyday computing, but it wasn't really any good for publishing. What was really required was a system with a printer that was truly whizzy-wig.

However, the first printer I came across was a 'dot matrix' printer. Dot matrix printing, sometimes called impact matrix printing, is a computer printing process in which ink is applied to a surface using a relatively low-resolution matrix of dots. Dot matrix printers typically use a print head that moves back and forth or in an up-and-down motion on the page and prints by impact, striking an ink-soaked cloth ribbon against the paper, much like the print mechanism on a typewriter or line printer.[14]

The trouble with the dot matrix printers that were around at the time was that they could only print out text. They were simple devices that chatted away in their own time when they had something to do, falling silent when they didn't. Although they were simple in relative terms, mine had perforated paper with holes punched along the margins to secure the paper in place. The paper came in continuous folded sheets harking back to the days of ticker-tape. The other issue was the density of type that wasn't very dense at all, and much like a typewriter, grew paler still as the ribbon wore out. For some reason, and I suppose there must be one, the paper had finely ruled green lines grouped at regular intervals across the central section of the paper. This was no good at all. Things did get better – and I'll explain that later, but I need first to say something about computer maintenance in these early days.

Computer maintenance

In the golden, olden days of the 80s and 90s computers could (and did) go wrong. They still do, but in my experience, not as much. Back then, they went wrong a lot. In fact, hardware engineers knew very well that they would go wrong because 'alerts' were built into the systems. If, or rather when, there was an error, a message would pop up pointedly informing you that 'Your Computer Has An Error' and yes, usually the message would appear with the initial letter of every word capitalized, perhaps for effect. It worked. Such was the tone of these messages that they implied that all errors were totally the responsibility of the user. Sometimes messages were more blatant. 'User Error' was common which I always thought was unfair. Not that I haven't made more than a few errors in my time, but none, I would suggest, were related to switching on a tired computer, particularly if I hadn't touched it since switching it off the day before.

The ultimate insult, of course was 'Your Computer Has A Fatal Error And Must Be Shut Down.' A bit rich given that when it displayed such a message it had usually done nothing other than woken up sluggishly, muttering "Wot-ever".

This kind of message intimated that the user had committed a crime nothing short of manslaughter. I always thought that 'fatal' was overdoing it a bit and besides, who or what was fated – me or the machine? Possibly neither, but it did mean that there was a big problem to fix.

I did once open the back of one of my early computers, not really expecting to fix it but thought that I could at least take a look. I'm sure it barked at me with a profanity I can't repeat; it clearly wanted to be left alone. I soon came to the conclusion that computer maintenance wasn't to be my forte. From then on I called in backup and have never again tried to mess with the mind of a motherboard.

Backup (the human type of backup) came in the form of a usually acned engineer of few years. They somehow had considerable experience and a passion for de-constructing the innards of computers. Hence, they had been hired to randomly distribute the components of my computer and those of my colleagues across our desks as we humbly grovelled for help.

Of course, I was grateful for the support. I would have been more grateful, however, if just for once, at such a crucial stage, my IT colleague had not decided to take a break for an extended lunch that lasted three days. On the third day, having tidied and re-tidied my office, not daring to touch the hung, drawn and quartered so-called computer, I decided to follow this up. I tried to do this as politely as I could knowing that an angry confrontation, or worse, the excessive use of sarcasm, would be counter-productive. But I failed.

"Had a nice lunch?" I clipped. This drew a blank. I took a different tack.
"About my computer ..."
A pause.
"What about your computer?" came a muffled reply.
"It's in pieces." I paused for effect. (Two could play at this game) ... "You took it apart."
"Ah, yes."
"Well do you think you could put it back together again? It's not Humpty Dumpty." (This remark also fell flat.)
"I suppose I could. Which building are you in?"
"The same building you found me in when you came to dissect my machine."
"OK, I'll be right with you."

It turned out that 'right with you' existed on a space-time continuum I was unfamiliar with but eventually he arrived. The components were reassembled, I presume correctly, as there were no more fatal errors for two weeks, at which point I was advised to upgrade.

Perhaps this account is unfair. All this was still new in most workplaces and IT staff also had to jump through technological hoops to be able to call themselves 'IT Support'.

Hardware was one half of the support. The other was software support. I rarely had an issue with the design software I used, but the operating system at the time (Windows 3.1) threw up a number of problems. Incidentally, I had really wanted to switch to the Apple Mac, but the University had decided to support only PCs and not Macs as they were pricey. The development of the top-end design programs for PCs, however, was several months, if not years, behind the development of programs running on the Mac which usually had fewer problems that needed fixing on a day-to-day basis.

Software support calls would always start with the ultimate and inevitable question:

"Have you made sure you have switched your computer off and on again?"

Now, I don't like to complain about this. It was protocol, I suppose. But it still confounds me. Why do I have to switch a computer off an on again to see if it works? Relate this point to, say, the aviation industry. Would you hear Air Traffic Control asking pilots to "switch it off and on again" – just to be sure? My guess is that you wouldn't.

Nevertheless, I said I had done that and again support arrived. Almost without exception, software support staff had minds that worked rather faster than their fingers. And also without exception the diminished keyboard skills resulting from this led to the backspace keys being worn down to a stub. They were good, but it was very painful to watch.

Happily, things are different now. At some point the University decided to devolve support to departments and employ support staff for each. The staff were dedicated as they are to this day. It worked well. We got to know each other and the pressures we were all under, whatever our roles, were shared and with this came mutual respect. Furthermore, we took lunch breaks at more or less the same time.

Another Vice-Chancellor later and it was decided to centralize computer services again. It hasn't been as bad as I feared as support requests are triaged and support is proffered by the appropriate member of staff who has the experience. How times have changed.

Desktop publishing

Shortly after starting work I came to understand what a desktop publishing system was or should be. On the back of an envelope I began to list the components of what might reasonably be called a desktop publishing system. I needed type, scanned graphics and images that could be compiled on the computer using a page layout program. The leading program was the aforementioned Aldus PageMaker. There was also Ventura Publisher and later QuarkXpress along with one or two others. These programs needed serious power and, as I was no way going back to the good old days of Gloy, the Amstrad had to go. This would make way for the new more powerful 286 computer.

I also needed a printer that could actually print out onto a white sheet of paper that would become the basis of the 'camera-ready-copy' – that is the design sheet that is used to create a printer's plate from. Laser printers were now on the market and in fact I had already used one. This was not a desktop item however, at least it wasn't on my desktop. It was based at the Computer Centre, a building about a mile away. I had recently discovered the joy of the 'file transfer protocol' (ftp) which could transfer a file across the university network to another computer or printer. Unfortunately, it couldn't transfer me as well. So to pick up the 'output' I had to get on my bike, often to find out when I got there that there was either a typo on the first page or else the printer had devilishly severed the bottom line of text horizontally leaving the ascenders on one page and the descenders on the next. Not helpful.

The advantage, however, is that the laser printer could print on A4 paper. The ink was dark and the characters crisp as they could be printed at a resolution of 300 dots per inch (dpi). Even today 300dpi is the standard resolution for desktop printing, rendering text and images crisply on up to A3 size documents. It still couldn't print out a whole page though. I could print out text and images in sections and piece them together on the physical pasteboard with Cow Gum. But this became tiresome not only as I spent the best part of the day cycling to and from the Computer Centre, but having trialled PageMaker at a desktop publishing convention at Earl's Court some months earlier, I knew another and better way was possible.

Bromides and the Linotronic

A desktop laser printer was a game-changer as far as office documentation and drafts of artwork were concerned. It became an essential piece of kit. However, printing onto 90 gram A4 recycled paper, though acceptable for everyday office use, still wasn't suitable when it came to making professional-standard printing plates for top quality print items. For this you needed 'bromides'. Bromide paper had been used for decades for producing photographic prints. The paper contains silver bromide that is sufficiently sensitive to light to produce ultra high definition plates. So, as a laser printer couldn't produce the definition at the resolution bromide paper could take, output to an 'imagesetter' was required. The 'Linotronic' was one of the leading brands of imagesetters, capable of printing at resolutions of up to 2540 dots per inch. It allowed the likes of me the possibility of cheaply creating camera-ready artwork that exceeded the quality of desktop printouts. The massive machines themselves, however, were anything but cheap, so to create the high-definition output I was after, I needed to get on my bike again, this time to a service bureau, with a file destined for print on a removable disk. Perhaps I should have added a new bike to my list of essential equipment required for desktop publishing.

A page description language

As was the way of things in the 1980s, technology advanced at a pace. Soon after purchasing the desktop publishing system (which included a laser printer) 'Postscript' came to the fore. Postscript is a page description language, or PDL, that describes the appearance of a printed page and not, in this case, an afterthought.

Postscript was conceived in the 1970s, but it took the founding of Adobe Systems in 1982 by John Warnock and Charles Geschke (the brains behind Postscript) and importantly the encouragement of Steve Jobs, for it to be adapted as the page description language for Apple Laserwriter printers and Linotronics. It was the natural choice as there were no real competitors.

As a page description language, Postscript finally nailed the issue of printing a page exactly as it appeared on the screen. WYSIWYG (What You See is What You Get) had finally arrived. I was joyful.

The reason Postscript was such a game-changer (a term I use unashamedly and repeatedly at various points throughout this story) is that Postscript converts elements on a page including text, to straight lines and curves geometrically. These are known as 'vector graphics'. In mathematics, a vector is what is needed to 'carry' lines from one point to another point. Points (sometimes called nodes) can plot the trajectory of particular shapes with exquisite precision and the shapes can be scaled without loss of definition. This is handy.

As it happens, throughout the course of my work I have created other types of vector graphics. Illustrations of living organisms that transmit infections, pathogens and viruses from animals to humans are also vector graphics of a kind. But here I only refer to computer- generated vectors.

The other type of *graphic* to note at this stage is the 'bitmap' or 'raster' graphic. Forgive me if I am teaching you, my grandmother, to suck eggs, but a bitmap is an image composed of a matrix of dots (or pixels) each assigned a particular colour. They too can be scaled but if enlarged they will lose definition as they aren't scaled geometrically in the same way as vector graphics. In extreme cases it is possible for the eye to identify the enlarged pixels of a bitmap graphic. If the image is reproduced at size, or smaller, the eye doesn't clock the pixels and the image appears harmoniously and pleasingly whole.

Postscript is clever because it grabs the vector graphics – once they are correctly sized and positioned on a page – and converts the vectors into bitmaps through a process known as 'rasterization'. The code generated from this process combined with other bitmap graphics form the page. The printer recognises the Postscript and prints the whizzy-wig page which is just brilliant. Brilliant, that is, if the printer does, in fact, recognise Postscript.

My printer, like most laser printers (with the exception of the Apple Laserwriter) didn't recognise Postscript. I could send part of a page to the Linotronic but I was still using a pasteboard to piece the final design together. My printer would make a calculated guess at what it thought a page should look like as much as the laser printer at the Computer Centre could do. It too could print out the page onto paper that no longer featured green lines placed at intervals across the page, and also print on to US Letter, A4 and other sizes including envelopes. The desktop laser printer would print using a few built-in typefaces and fonts which, for documents composed exclusively of text, meant that the printer could print across pages as it fancied which wouldn't be too much of a problem and was still a big improvement to the look of office documents.

However, for camera-ready artwork, it didn't cut it because text and images featured in most designs and had to be located precisely in their intended positions. I needed the Postscript code and send it to a Postscript printer for drafting and to a Linotronic for final output.

By now there was a Postscript printer installed at the Computer Centre and a Linotronic with a Postscript driver at the service bureau. Back on my bike again.

First of all, I would cycle up to the Computer Centre to collect the Postscript drafts which eventually I put together entirely with PageMaker which had its own comforting virtual pasteboard to work with. There was a problem, however. A stream of Postscript code has to begin with two key characters: the percentage sign followed by an exclamation mark (%!). This lets the printer know that a Postscript file is on its way and prevents the printer from going off piste, keeping it on track to print the page as instructed.

For a reason that I never understood, however, was that the Postscript code I generated in the office always lacked the first two essential characters at the top of the file. Whilst it was easy enough to send the file to the Computer Centre, not only did I have to cycle there to pick up the output, I also had to edit the code before letting it print and add the two key symbols to the file so, that when eventually I did hit 'Print', it would behave as it should.

Woe betide me if I ever forgot to edit the essential code as I did on more than one occasion. The file would print for sure, but it would excrete only the code – every single page of the verbose code spewing out into the output tray as though the printer had a severe bout of papered diarrhoea for which there was no technological equivalent of Imodium. I tried switching the printer off and on again (of course I did) but that didn't work. When the printer was off, the code would sit there quietly and patiently waiting for its moment to strike, like troops waiting for the call to battle. Switching the printer on again, pages, and pages and pages, like military reinforcements, charged with such shock and awe I could have cried. And its unending call to battle: "attack-attack; attack-attack; attack-attack; attack-attack", drove me to despair.

But hope sprung from the depths of despair. Postscript developed to a third level and then, finally, joyously, the child of Postscript was born: The Portable Document Format – PDF.

PDF

Based on Postscript, again it was John Warnock of Adobe Systems, a company now inflating as quickly as had The Big Bang, who developed the portable document format. Warnock led The Camelot Project which worked it out. As legendary as King Arthur is, PDF emerged in 1992, not centuries ago.

So like Postscript, a PDF file is one which can present a page including all its elements – images, vector and bitmap graphics, text and their associated attributes including typefaces and fonts. The key difference is that a PDF is independent of application software, hardware and operating systems. Whereas, latterly, Postscript printer drivers were required to enable the printing of Postscript on non-Postscript printers, PDFs did away with all that faff. My goal has always been to approach work in an efficient and effective manner, so this was all very good. Nowadays, PDF files can also contain content beyond images and text and include interactive layers, and even videos. With Adobe Acrobat, the generator of PDF files, there are a number of tools available for editing, page organisation, security and a whole lot more. But at first it simply made getting documents to the printers so much easier. It was another game-changer, not only for designers, but for everyone.

It took a while to catch on, but Adobe made a canny move in 2008 by making the specification of the portable document format free of charge and it was standardized as ISO 32000.[15] Naturally the format grew exponentially as the Adobe Acrobat Reader was available for all operating systems including Windows, MacOS, Unix and others and was free to download. It propelled Adobe stage-centre to join Microsoft and Apple in their crusade to dominate personal computing worldwide.

As with many new software and application developments, the portable document format mutated in several ways. PDF/X for example, is a subset of the PDF ISO Standard which includes a number of printing-related requirements which don't apply to standard PDF files. For colour printing that uses four colours (cyan, magenta, yellow and black – CMYK) or specifically purposed spot colours (solid colours mixed to be independent of the CMYK colour process) there are other standards.

There is more I could write about PDFs but it's not all that interesting and I've already gone as far as mentioning ISO standards which is not the best way, I fear, to keep you reading on. So I'll leave it there, suffice to say that the tricky business of CMYK colour separation is no longer my problem. Now I just create a PDF file and send it to print. Job done.

Adobe

Adobe, however, is worth more mention as there are millions of users of their products across the globe and, if indeed you have managed to read this far, you are probably one of them – even if you are just saving Word files as PDFs.

Along the way, Adobe has gobbled up a number of smaller companies to create an extensive suite of design and publishing software for print and online which is unrivalled. It also has its head in the iCloud, a subject I'll return to later.

It wasn't long after PageMaker had reached its eleventh edition that Adobe took it over and it became Adobe InDesign. The first version was littered with bugs that it looked like QuarkXpress would become the dominant page layout program. It did for a while, but Adobe stepped up to the mark with innovations and, importantly bug fixes, to the extent that I don't hear much about QuarkXpress anymore although it is still around and I suspect has been upgraded too.

Alongside InDesign was Photoshop. This is a great program, used by many to enhance poor quality images or crop people who are no longer friends out of pictures. But it does more. There are many similar products today that perform well, but Photoshop has become an old friend so I stick with it.

Adobe Illustrator also features in my top three list of Adobe products. It is used for designing vector graphics. Illustrator complements Photoshop which is a pixel based program. As I had trained as a fine artist, I resisted at first to take a computer-based approach to technical illustration seriously. I preferred to sketch everything freehand instead but over time, I did eventually realise that once more the computer was the right tool for the job.

All the same, with an increasing workload, I called in a pro who produced beautiful technical illustrations at lightening speed. I was in awe. He had previously worked for Volvo, illustrating exploded diagrams of engines, animating them and doing much else.

Of course I wanted a go, so when I had time I dabbled and became hooked. It took a long time, but I am reasonably competent and the work I have done for the World Health Organization (WHO) has gone down well. This sounds boastful, but I should add that I had a remarkable mentor who has become a good friend, as too has his wife who produces astonishing botanical illustrations I am equally in awe of.

But now to rewind a little. I return to earlier days and the extremely painful experience of buying a computer.

Buying computers

These days, it is quite easy to buy computers. You can buy them online or from a computer shop. You can also buy them from superstores where all you have to do is find the right aisle amongst the many aisles of washing machines, dishwashers, cameras, vacuum cleaners, microwaves and all other white goods. You pick one up, then go and pay. Well, almost. You may ponder for a while to run through those nagging doubts about its suitability and whether a new and better model will be launched the very moment you pass through the checkout. By this point, although rarely these days, an assistant may have sidled up to you and joined you in your contemplation asking you quietly if they could help you out. They may wait with you as you stare at the box with an intensity rivalling that of shepherds doting on the Baby Jesus. I'm never quite sure if this is a proven sales tactic or a means of assistants making themselves look busy. Either way it works. Apple have got it down to a fine art, letting you play with the range of products so it's hard to leave the store without one.

But it never used to be like that. Before I bought the first computer for myself I had to study and evaluate desktop systems in some depth as they were expensive. That was reasonable enough as with any new technology there can be huge differences in function and reliability. It used to be the same with fridges, but now the technology of the fridge is well established, the only real differences are in style, gadgets and capacity as they all keep things cool.

Research took me once more to Earl's Court and a sales convention that was packed with computers, printers, scanners and peripherals all rapidly evolving, seemingly from one day to the next. It was the age of the 'Yuppie' and 'Loads of Money'. It was all very bewildering. Where to start?

I decided to consider what it was I was actually trying to achieve with a desktop publishing system, then I would be able to choose one to suit. The trouble was that I had to get to my head around the terminology of the insides of a computer so that I could make sure that it featured the mother of all motherboards running at maximum speed with the maximum amount of 'random access memory – RAM.' And what on earth was that?

Of course I didn't buy anything there and then. I'm one of those people who will always end a sales conversation with "I'll think about it." I shopped around and bought the computer, the printer and the scanner piecemeal. I used the system for about a year until it was time for another upgrade. For this, two sales representatives arrived at work, caked in makeup and wearing high heels. Their attire was in marked contrast to my own somewhat casual dress code. Nevertheless, they had come up with the right goods. I thanked them profusely and said I would think about it.

I did think about it and their van driver soon returned with big boxes. They were big because desktop computers, still manufactured with cathode tubes, were becoming bigger as monitors grew in size. They were bulbous beasts, driven largely from a universal desire for a better resolution of a page design on a screen. Later on in the story, with flat screens you could buy a computer that, like a cat, would sit on your lap and purr. By then, the days of the first cute cuboid Macs were long gone.

Upgrading

The purchase of the 286 computer was in effect my first upgrade. It felt like a milestone. It could handle the software I was using at the time, had a good working relationship with the printer and did all this much more quickly than the Amstrad which was now sat forlorn and redundant. And herein lay the problem. Countless machines were becoming obsolete. The environmental impacts of building computers using precious natural resources and then the disposal of them within an unreasonably short amount of time were huge. Quite how huge an issue this was I couldn't be sure, but it troubled me. I had an existential crisis on my hands. To upgrade or not to upgrade, that was the question. Not an easy one to answer at that.

Inevitably, and to some extent reluctantly, and to further extent shamefully and gleefully, I upgraded. As software developed to make the process of work more efficient, it required more powerful machines that had plenty of memory, bigger hard disks and faster processors. Self-induced guilt was ramped up every year as the industry kept on developing hardware and software with higher and higher specifications. Of course, the prime purpose of the major multinationals was to line the pockets of their shareholders, and I was well aware of this. But there were genuine advancements that were hard to ignore. They were mainly about speed and memory: power and performance in other words.

The 286 was so called after the Intel 80286, a 16 bit microprocessor. Wikipedia describes it as "the first 8086-based CPU with separate, non-multiplexed address and data buses and also the first with memory management and wide protection abilities."[16] I've no idea what this means but it does highlight the complexity of knowing precisely what it was you were buying and whether or not it was a sound investment.

After the 286 came the 386 and I now had the equivalent computing power that took man to the moon. So surely this would be sufficient for me to design a few leaflets and maybe even the odd book?

But then came the 486 and then the Pentium. Then I lost track of further manifestations of the computer that were more powerful still as time went on. These computers were all PCs. But despite my reservations about upgrading, I still hankered after an Apple Mac. Windows computers are fine and they are more fine now than they used to be, but the software still lagged behind what was available for the Mac. Early on, the Mac had other innovative characteristics PCs lacked and they were attractive to look at. Later, they came in different colours and this attention to design detail also featured in the way the operating system worked. This was mainly down to the obsessive mindset of Steve Jobs, even though he lost his job along the way only to be reinstated some years later because Apple couldn't do without him. He employed top designers who paid equal attention to form as to function.

Upgrading remains a perennial issue today. Whereas upgrading used to be about making work easier and more efficient, it is now, as with smartphones, about status too. For some, upgrading is addictive. Folk camp out to get their hands on the newest, latest device. It's not for me to pass judgement, but it does remind me to stay grounded and true to my earlier instincts that there should be sound reasons for upgrading, however lovely new things look.

Windows 95

It was not only hardware that needed upgrading, it was software too. With Windows 95 came the start-up jingle.

I've never really seen the point of jingles, particularly those designed for computers. The Windows 95 jingle was composed by no other than Brian Eno, he of the 1970s glam-rock band Roxy Music and since a prolific musician and record producer. I had always liked Roxy Music and was an admirer of Eno's solo albums. Even his ambient music was kind of interesting. But a jingle? Not Eno? It lasted for six seconds[17]. I haven't dared count how many times over the years I must have sat listening to it. How many days, weeks or months of my life have I waited and wasted whilst Windows cranked up? Originally the jingle was supposed to be three and a half seconds long, so where did the other two and a half seconds come from? What is neatly ironic though, is that Eno composed the wretched sound on a Mac and at this point had never actually owned a PC. Nowadays, on YouTube, you can find the jingle slowed down to last for an hour[18]. Why would anybody do this? It might be pushing the boundaries of muzak forward, but I can think of many other more important pursuits such as providing two plus billion people with a safe place to defecate or combating terrorism and climate change, just for starters.

To continue this rant a little: why have a start-up jingle in the first place? It's not as if they are particularly pleasant to listen to. Hadn't the very notion of a start-up given way by the 1980s? No longer did televisions need to warm up. You could switch one on and there, in a flash, was the sound and the picture.

Great. But now the future is here, we are once more confronted with start-ups and hour-glasses, whirligigs and time bars all designed to comfort us and reassure us that something important is happening when all we want to do is to get on.

Text and typography

It goes without saying that for both print and online documents, text is a key component of a page design – to a greater or lesser extent depending on the nature of the document.

Typography is about what text looks like or more precisely 'the art and technique of arranging type to make written language legible, readable and appealing when displayed'[19]. There is much to say about it in the way it relates to desktop publishing.

My initial interest in what text look liked, however, was when I learnt to read and write, as it would have been for most people. Forming letters is difficult at first but over time and with the drill of practice it gets better. We all know this. I developed quite a neat hand at school and actually won the penmanship prize three years running, but that was because nobody else entered the competitions.

There was another aspect of text that also interested me as a boy, apart from the aforementioned Letraset and a typewriter, and that was punching letters onto a plastic adhesive strip using a handheld device called a

Dymo Tape Machine. With this I could create labels for things. If I remember rightly, the letters were only available as capitals, and grammar marks consisted of commas and full stops. Maybe an apostrophe too. Nevertheless, I got very excited about it. I created labels for a range of items whether it was necessary for them to have a label or not. Usually not. One of these was 'ROD'S TIN' even though I knew full well that it was my tin. My parents and my brother knew it was my tin too, but now, I thought, there was no mistaking it. I have to say that I was a little disappointed, that having mastered the technology of the punch, my Mum felt that labels for the kettle, the fridge, the oven and the pantry weren't strictly necessary either. As for my tin, inside it I kept random boyhood items ranging from segs that were no longer fashionable to dry conkers and a plaster cast of a severed finger I had sculpted using a Christmas present called 'Replica'. The usual things. Looking back, the tin was the precursor to my 'man box', which curiously has a label on it telling me that too. To defend myself here, there are a number of similar boxes which contain other things, so labelling it does have a purpose. I have grown-up items in the man box now, but alas, no longer the segs or the fake, severed finger.

It is a bitter irony though, that in later years I did indeed return to labelling things around the house. My Dad's house. He lived with dementia after my mum had passed away and at first the labels (made this time by hand on A4 paper) helped him, but they too became redundant eventually.

So my interest in typography goes back a long way and has been, and still is, ever present. Prior to the explosion of desktop publishing, the typefaces available at the time for designers and printers were relatively modest in number, at least by today's standards. With the introduction of the first Mac onto the market, things changed. Again, it was Steve Jobs who captured the zeitgeist. He had taken calligraphy classes ten years earlier and became captivated by the arrangements of letters and words, and the nature of typefaces too.

Jobs took a great deal of care over the design of these new typefaces. Seemingly overnight the number available to Mac users had increased exponentially. The first were used to display text on the graphical user interface (GUI) and so were somewhat pixelated, but they worked. 'Chicago' was used for all the menus and dialog boxes that featured on the Mac. Jobs liked to call these new typefaces after his favourite cities: Geneva, Toronto, Venice and Los Angeles, for example, the latter two having a handwritten quality to them. Due to their pixelated nature, however, they are now consigned to history, but this period heralded a 'seismic shift in our everyday relationship with letters and type'. This quote comes from *Just My Type*, a book about fonts by Simon Garfield. If you need to know more about them, this is a good place to start.[20]

My own relationship with letters and type certainly changed with the advent of desktop publishing. It had raised the bar when it came to using type, but it came with a downside too. Now everyone was using a whole range of typefaces for everyday use and many of the results were ghastly with every typeface published to date featuring on posters, invitations and stationery. As a designer, I can happily accept that less is more and that to be taken seriously as a designer means never, ever using Comic Sans.

There was a lot to learn with the bar raised. First of all, the difference between a typeface and a font. They are used interchangeably, but I thought I needed to get my head around this. For the record, a typeface is the 'parent' name for fonts that are aligned with it. So 'Helvetica' is a typeface, but 'Helvetica Bold', being a 'child' of Helvetica, is a font'. 'Helvetica, 12pt' is a font too as the point size is a defined aspect of Helvetica.

There were also many other aspects of typography terminology I needed to get the hang of: leading (the space between lines); kerning (the tweaking of character spaces); glyphs (hieroglyphic characters or symbols); grep (global regular expression print – a means of applying a character style to override a paragraph style); widows and orphans (a widow – the end of a paragraph which has a single line of text consisting of one or more words appearing at the top of a column; an orphan – a single word or syllable that sits at the bottom of a paragraph of text, neither of which is all that easy to avoid); ligatures (occurring where two or more letters are joined to form a single glyph. e.g. ae). The list goes on, but I won't, only to say that although all these aspects of typography seem very pedantic, collectively they can make for a rather nice arrangement of text if used judiciously. If done well, you shouldn't really notice them, unless, like me, you are keeping a look out for them.

Email and the Internet

Something really cool

One day in the early 1990s I had an unsolicited visitor arrive from the Computer Centre. I had seen him before and knew that when it came to anything to do with computing he didn't suffer fools gladly, so I was a little nervous.

"I have something really cool to show you."

At the time I universally disliked people who used 'cool' to describe things. (I use it all the time now.)

"Cool is it?", I ventured.

"Dead cool", he replied, unmoved.

"Go on then, what have you got?"

"I'll show you. You have to let me at your computer though ... have you saved everything?"

"Yes, I think so," I replied with growing concern. But by this point he had already started to install a new application.

"So what's that you've got?" I asked reasoning that I had a right to know what was going on.

"It's called Eudora."

"OK, and what does Eudora do?" I asked with muted interest.

"It's like MailShare."

"OK. And what does 'MailShare' do?"

"It shares mail."

"Right."

"Here we go. Type a message here," he continued, undeterred.

"What message do you want me to type?"

"Whatever you like. Ask me if I'm having a nice day. Go on. No, not there ... THERE! ... now type the name of the recipient here and press send."

"Hang on a minute." I puzzled. "Surely I also need to enter a destination? How does your clever Eudora thingy do that?"

"It uses an email address," he stated calmly.

"Email?"

"Electronic mail."

"So you are telling me that I can send you an electronic message to a ... what is it ... an email address?"

"Yes."

"Forgive me, I'm missing something here. If I wanted to ask you if you were having a nice day I could do that now, so why would you want to wait for a message from me saying as much when you get back to your office? Sounds a bit long-winded to me. And if you weren't here and I wanted to ask you if you were having a nice day, I would ring you."

"But what if I wasn't in?"

"I'd try again later."

"And what if I wasn't in for the rest of the day?"

"I'd try again tomorrow. I'm sorry but I really don't see any advantage in going to the trouble of writing you a message when all I have to do is phone you up instead."

"You'll see." And with that he left.

Email – then and now

Eventually, of course, I did see. Today, on a normal working day I write to or reply to about thirty emails, sometimes more. It's hard to think about life without email, and despite my initial scepticism, within the week I did concede that email might be useful for the occasional message.

Before too long I was sending a lot, and to begin with, it was manageable. I continued to use the phone, but an email, I discovered, could be sent to the recipient who could let you know that they had seen it with a 'read receipt'. This happened all the time until we all found that annoying and stopped doing it.

Things started to get out of hand when it became possible to attach a file to an email and as though by magic, the same document would copy itself and turn up elsewhere. This was 'cool' at first. Bear in mind that the only other way of doing this at the time was by fax. Fax machines could send and receive a paper message containing images, graphics – anything that a photocopier could copy. So a fax could include handwriting, sketches and diagrams. Apart from the overly thin and shiny paper, it was perfect for sending one or two pages. But over time the print would fade and the paper degrade.

It so happened that around this time I had been involved with developing a distance learning programme. As a paper-based course, it would be possible to send copies of distance learning materials pretty much anywhere in the world. The trouble here though was that I hadn't clocked that one of the first students on the course was located on St Helena, a small island that peeked its peak out of the middle of the Atlantic Ocean, so remote that Napoleon was exiled there. Posting the course materials was not going to be easy. The package would need to catch one of the monthly sailings from Cardiff to Angola, and hang around there for a while until there was a sailing from Angola to the island. At that time there was no airport on St Helena.

As I dropped the package into the post I knew that this wasn't going to end well. It didn't. On the day the course started I spent the best part of the day faxing page after page of the materials to the student in the hope that they had enough rolls of fax paper to print it all out at the other end.

So the idea of attaching a document to a message was initially very appealing. There is a problem with this, however. Everything you have to say can be written in the message and everything you want to refer to can be attached. The message and attachment can be sent not only to the intended recipient but also to other recipients who more often than not will have less than a passing interest in it. What's more, if you send a message relating to a task of work with which you are involved, then it is off your desk. Not your problem anymore. If the recipient failed to be diligent and did not attend to the task at hand and contacted the sender to enquire about its status, the usual reply would be: "Well I sent you an email." This is just annoying.

Whether we like it or not, emails are a fact of working life. Despite the convenience of sending messages electronically, there is no one I know who doesn't complain about receiving too many. You never hear anyone ever say they wished they'd had a few more emails that day. On return from leave, the first job is always to 'deal' with the email though much of it is 'spam'. It's relatively easy to spot spam, particularly if you're invited to try out a state-of-the-art incontinence pad when, as yet, you don't need one; or you receive a request to send money to an overseas bank account for no clear reason. Even so, there are many more messages that lurk like woodlice under a garden stone only to be revealed when you scroll down the page of your inbox. And what do I do? Of course, I put the stone back.

I have always found signing off emails to be problematic. Protocol precludes 'Yours sincerely' or 'Yours faithfully'. Either would be too formal though as something of a traditionalist in this respect I am comfortable using either of them for letters, though I hardly ever write letters anymore. 'Yours' may just about be acceptable for emails but at work I send emails to recipients I don't necessarily know all that well, if indeed at all, so I'm blowed if I'm going to be 'theirs'.

Sometimes I use 'Best wishes' if I can genuinely mean it though just 'Best' I dislike as it strikes me as lazy, and when you think about it, somewhat ambiguous without the addition of the wishes. Best what? Best birthday ever; best lunch I've had in years; best go reply to my other emails?

I usually settle for sending regards, distributing them in liberal quantities like a pre-industrial sower scattering seeds randomly in the hope that some might land in the right furrow. In fact, I usually send *kind* regards and what is a regard if it isn't kind? That I worry about this tells me I should get out more.

The Internet

I called this narrative *What You See Is What You Get* as WYSIWYG was the Holy Grail when I first started to use a computer for design and print. With Postscript and PDF I thought I had found it and up to a point I had. But then something big was just around the corner which would reset the button on whizzy-wig: The Internet.

I was brought up in a house which had a telephone in the hall. As far as I was concerned it was just a part of everyday life, a great device for chatting and making arrangements to play with mates. That it hadn't always been the case was born out by how my parents spoke into the receiver loudly. If the call was international, they would speak even louder to be sure that the listener could hear. To them, the telephone at home was still a relatively modern gadget. Similarly, if you are over a certain age, you will remember that there was a time when there wasn't the Internet and when it arrived, thought that perhaps it would be no more than a convenient curiosity bringing with it one or two marginal benefits for modern living.

I first came across the Internet in much the same way as I had come across email. It would be around 1993. I had put in a request call for help with a computer maintenance issue and the same engineer that had introduced me to email turned up.

"I've got something to show you," he said excitedly. "And what might that be this time?" I enquired with a foreboding sense of déjà vu.

"Let me show you," he said, whisking the mouse out of my hand and tapping vigorously on the keyboard.

"There!"

"And...?"

"It's a picture."

"I see that."

"It's come from America."

"I'm sure many do, America's not exactly the back of beyond."

"Ah yes! But I've downloaded this one."

"You've done what?"

"Downloaded it."

"You're going to have to explain," I said conceding that I really had no idea what he was on about and still rather hoping that instead, he might fix the software problem I had.

"Well, it was uploaded in America and I've just downloaded it."

I was none the wiser. "Sorry, could you go back a step please?"

"Well..." he started, noting that he needed to explain everything slower and in more detail.

"You know about FTP – the File Transfer Protocol?"

"Yes," I said. "I can send a file to the Computer Centre and then cycle over and pick up the printout. Is this like that?"

"Sort of."

"Which bit of 'sort of' isn't it like?"

"You don't need a bike. Or a boat. Or an aircraft for that matter. You see, there are other types of protocol you might be interested in. The Transmission Control Protocol (TCP) and the Internet Protocol (IP), usually grouped together so known as 'TCP/IP' for short."

"Mmm," I replied thinking that I really didn't want to get involved in any more protocols than I had to, but as I could see he was going to persist, I continued.

"And so you used these protocols to offload this picture?" I said.

"Download it – yes."
"From America? Just now?"
"You got it!"

I hadn't. How could this possibly be? Of course, I knew that files could be sent from place to place, but on further enquiry, I found that there was no central place where this or any other image resided. It was a network of computers all seemingly connected to each other. Clearly, he had connected mine to a network at some point. In fact, although I wasn't aware of it at the time, every computer on the campus was connected to the Joint Academic Network or JANET for short. And JANET was connected to another network. I would like to think that this other network was called JOHN, but that could never be as JANET was part of a network of networks. Collectively this was called the 'Internet', although initially for the likes of me, the Internet (or was it Inter-Net) was only ever seen to be a way of sending and receiving emails.

The Internet has been so called from its earliest manifestation in the late 1970s, a child of the United States Department of Defense's 'Defense Advanced Research Projects Agency', should you need to know. My own interest in the Internet was heightened at the point at which I tried it out for myself. I became an advocate and as best I could, I explained it to others in the group to try and convince them that the network of networks might actually change the way of work in years to come. One of the administrators was unconvinced and it's not hard to see why. It was new. As she had an interest in tennis, she challenged me to find out what the scores were in a tournament that was taking place in New York at that moment. I had just discovered that there was a means of finding out what was on the Internet and that was called a 'search engine' and sure enough I found the results in real-time and gave them to her. She didn't seem convinced of their authenticity. "I'll check them on Ceefax later," she said, "...and if they're right, I'll check tomorrow's on your inter thing."

Two years later in 1995, I presented a paper at the 21st WEDC International Conference in Kampala, Uganda. Since WEDC was formed in 1971, it has been committed to keeping alumni, their sponsors and other stakeholders in touch with current activities and new initiatives. It disseminates the results of its research and shares the experiences gained from consultancy assignments undertaken in many low- and middle-income countries throughout the world. It was for this reason that I figured that I should see if I could make use of the Internet to advance these aims. I was bold and a little naive like that.

The original vision for the Internet was that it was to provide the opportunity of maintaining communication with as much of the world as possible, should any region or country be devastated by war. The advantage of an international network based on TCP/IP is that it is decentralized, so multiple computer file servers across the world can maintain the links between organizations and institutions that have offices in other countries without necessarily being dependent on a central system. This point seems evident today, but networks were becoming a big thing and the Internet was going to be a really big thing. With the threat of global nuclear war diminished since the end of the Cold War, the Internet started to be adopted by academic institutions and businesses. Email was the primary function but then a new, transformative way of using the Internet joined the party. The World Wide Web.

The World Wide Web

Tim-Berners-Lee, a graduate of Oxford University, invented the WorldWideWeb; (initially it was one word). When I first heard about this I found it difficult to accept that a single person could invent a computer system that would *actually* change the world. But that's just about what he did, although the underlying concept of 'hypertext' (text which contains links to other texts) originated in previous projects from the 1960s, and after the draft concept was proposed, other enthusiasts came on board too. This was in 1989 when Tim-Berners-Lee was working at CERN, the European Particle Physics Laboratory. In 1990, a more formal proposal included the notion of the 'web client', now more commonly known as the 'browser'. This, as I am sure you know, allows a user to interact with the content delivered from the 'Web' via a 'web server'. A web server is a server that runs the 'Hypertext Transfer Protocol' (HTTP for short). Tim-Berners-Lee and friends also specified the format for Uniform Resource Locators (URLs) and 'HTML' the 'Hypertext Mark-up Language'. There is much more to this than I have explained here, but essentially, with a web client, a web server, a language and a protocol, the World Wide Web was all ready to go.

And did it go! Whilst the Internet was created for a military purpose, the World Wide Web could be used by anyone with a bit of know-how. But it wasn't until 1993 that the Web began to seep into mainstream academia although the business community and pornographers had seized on it much earlier.

In 1993, I wrote my first HTML code and though I can hardly admit to it now, it did seem at least a little bit exciting. This was, after all, the beginning of something that was going to be big. HTML resembled the code I had first used for word processing. I don't remember the HTML code precisely, but it would be along these lines:

<html><head>
<title> <bold>The Water, Engineering and Development Centre </bold></title>
</head><body>

```
<p><center>Welcome to the Water, Engineering and
Development Centre at Loughborough University.
</center></p>
</body></html>
```

Again, like the code for word processing, in browser mode, it read thus:

The Water, Engineering and Development Centre

Welcome to the Water, Engineering and Development Centre at Loughborough University.

As you can imagine, this was quite a faff. But although the code looks grim, because it was similar to word processing, there was a natural progression from writing documents to writing web pages. Displayed in a browser, the HTML code was, in a sense, truly WYSIWYG – what you see is what you get. In another sense, it wasn't, because what you saw is not what you necessarily wanted to see. The simple display of a basic page was so far removed from the polished print documents that I was beginning to produce that it felt underwhelming.

The main issue was that everything was presented on a grey background. There were a limited number of typefaces that could be used and an angled line would be rendered in pixels, so it would assume the form of a staircase and not really a sraight line at all. This issue was even more marked with curves. I got around this by not using curves, but for a graphic artist, this was an aberration. It's hard to believe that the first pages I produced looked like this. HTML developed progressively and fast with the W3 Consortium setting international standards for HTML code at every turn. But in the beginning, that grey background was just frustrating. It's here where I need to mention BOND, not James Bond, but a recently formed (real world) network.

BOND

WEDC at Loughborough University is not a non-governmental organization (NGO) but throughout its history, much work has been centred around issues that NGOs deal with at the coalface of international development and emergencies, particularly the provision of water supply and sanitation in low- and middle-income countries. As such, it has established links with, for example, WaterAid and Practical Action, (formerly the Intermediate Technology Development Group). On the back of this, I got a ticket to a gig – a meeting of British Overseas NGOs for Development – BOND which was about the potential of the Web to further its mission.

The discussions that took place at this meeting were not all about technology, but these were the ones that interested me most and was the reason I pitched up. I was by no means in the minority when it came to designing web pages with the intent of doing good. We were all trying to wrestle with this new technological kid on the block (i.e. the Web). What's more, none of us liked grey backgrounds.

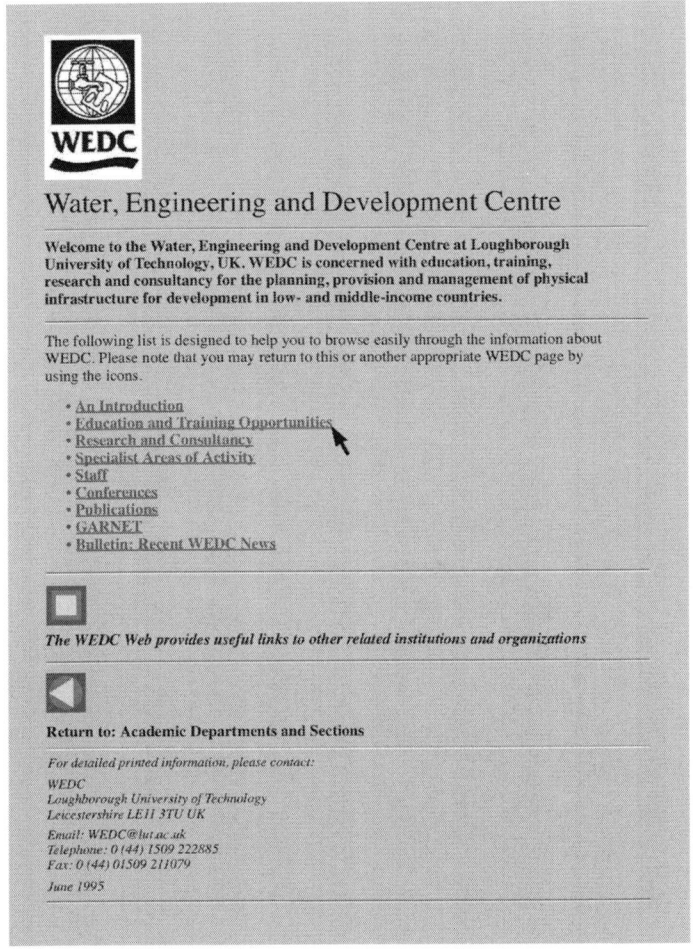

Figure 14. The 'home' page of the first version of the WEDC website, 1995

It so happened that the BBC was represented at this meeting too. It was quite an honour to be introduced to the Beeb's entire website development team. All three of them. What was even more exciting was that they had figured out how to develop a web page that had a *white* background.

It would have been fair for Tim Berners-Lee to have rested on his laurels after having invented the Web. It was a big deal. But he didn't. With further insight, he formed The World Wide Web Consortium (W3C) as an international community to develop open standards that would ensure the long-term growth and longevity of the Web. This was almost as important as the invention of the Web itself. W3C attempted to foster and promote the compatibility of code that would ensure that it would render in the same way on the myriad of browsers that were being developed by third-party vendors. This was significant as such vendors were developing their own extensions of code for their browsers with little regard as to whether it would work on other browsers. This was very dim. What it meant was that what you saw on one browser was not what you saw on another. Herein came my second whizzy-wig challenge.

Over the years W3C has tried to reel in the rogue vendors and their code and it has mainly succeeded. But in the early days, it was necessary to code for one browser, say Netscape, and cross-check it against, say, Internet Explorer. The two were rarely the same. It may seem like nothing, but nudging text over to the next line when it shouldn't can make a page look like a dog's dinner.

For these reasons, I ultimately realised that I no longer wanted to become a web developer as tussling with code was not how I wanted to spend my working life. Thankfully a new type of IT species had evolved – people who relished the challenge and who were eminently capable of overcoming these issues without losing sleep. They were 'The Webmasters'.

At around this time, I had moved into a management role. When it came to managing the WEDC website, I found that a partnership between myself (obsessively concerned with design) and the Webmaster (obsessively concerned with code) was fruitful. Of course, there were tussles of a friendly nature between what was desirable and what was possible and reasonable. This compromising approach usually resulted in a decent piece of work.

Alongside the developments in design and technology, there were discussions at BOND and elsewhere about what the Web could do for international development and what it couldn't. It was at the conference in Uganda in 1995 where I raised this issue. As chance would have it, the first Internet connection had just been installed in the Sheraton Hotel in Kampala, and there was real interest in the Web at the conference. It was less of a side show than I had expected it to be. This somewhat raised the stakes when I got up to speak as I was really no expert on either the Internet or the World Wide Web and only an inch ahead of the game than the rest of the delegates. Thankfully I managed to respond to questions about the technology well enough and found that "I'll have to get back to you on that one" a useful retort, one of my favourites to this day.

I had actually hoped to nudge the discussion around what the benefits the Web had for development, and not to focus on the technology side of things, but that was less successful. All the same, I recorded my views in the paper and reflecting back I wonder whether for once, I had been right about the future, at least in part. The conclusions to the paper at this, the 21st WEDC International Conference were as follows:

> "Despite the limitations of electronic-based media, and the additional fear that the Internet may be dominated in the future by multinational corporations demanding payment for access to their data, the World Wide Web presents a growing percentage of those who have a genuine desire to build a better world with a new and exciting means of cooperation and collaboration. Within its own context, the Web is truly democratic. It has no hierarchy, and there is, as yet, no censorship. Of course, there is the potential to misinform, to fuel bias and to corrupt, but this has always been the case with mass-communication media.

In 1932, Berthold Brecht lamented the limitations of broadcasting:

'What a wonderful apparatus broadcasting could be if it would only receive as well as transmit, make the recipient speak instead of just listen, relate him to others, instead of isolating him from them.'

The Web experiment is a step towards the realization of Brecht's dream. One World Online [a leading website of the time] hopes to take a further step forward at the end of this year by offering NGOs the opportunity of introducing audio and video clips to their sites. Video conferencing is on the agenda for the next millennium when people in different parts of the world will be able to participate in live audio and visual discussions.

The long-term success of the World Wide Web as a serious communication tool for sustainable development, however, will ultimately depend on the widespread introduction of low-cost connections in the South, and on the generous and regular provision of appropriate and accessible information for all."

In 2021, due to the raging COVID-19 pandemic, the 42nd WEDC International Conference was hosted entirely online, accessible from a web-based platform, for 600 delegates dialling in from 42 countries. I managed the conference from my dining room.

Search engines

From the outset, it was clear that there needed to be a way of finding out what there was on the Web. I had used a rudimentary search engine to find out the tennis results for my colleague but as the Web progressed, so did the development of search engines.

In essence, a search engine is a software system that returns a series of results from a web query, as I'm sure you will know. But what is less known is how they came to be. Search *systems* had been envisaged long before computers landed on our desktops. In 1945 Vannevar Bush, an American engineer and science administrator saw the need for filing research data and documentation in a way that could be quickly retrieved.[21] He proposed the connection of annotations between documents. This approach to 'link analysis' formed the basis of the development of hyperlinks, the difference being that computers perform such analyses much more quickly. But how? If I enter a search term such as 'Monet's late paintings' the results show up in the blink of an eye.

Well, as I understand it, and perhaps you do too, behind the scenes, a search term is listed in an index. A search engine will have created this list by trawling the entire web using an algorithm that filters the results. It doesn't actually search the web every time; it just looks up a search term in its index. This index may well be duplicated across multiple sites in mirrored data centres.

All the same, this doesn't actually answer my central question about why it does it so quickly. I've tried finding out by, ironically, searching the Web. I noticed with some consternation that unless very specific terms are used, a search engine will throw out reams of results with a resounding: "There you are .... well you did ask."

So this is evidently a case of 'What You Ask For Is Not Necessarily What You Get'. I did enter what I thought was a reasonable and specific query: "Why are search engines so fast?" and a number of results were duly returned but I couldn't find the answer from any of the suggested links. Deciding that life is too short, I regressed to my toddler self and accepted the parental reply to why questions: "It's because."

In the 1990s, of all the search engines that were vying for dominance, that is to say, Achie, Gopher, Vernica, Jughead, Wanderer, Aliweb, Worm, WebCrawler, JumpStation, Yahoo!, Altavista, Ask Jeeves and many more it is Google, of course, whose brand name became the verb. To google.

Why Google is so dominant, pulling in over two-thirds of all web searches, is because the company has spent a fortune trying to create a system that supplies the *best* search results quickly. It took a qualitative as well as a quantitative approach focusing on the relationship between links as well as the results. Google stones you with thousands of results and they are focused if you choose the right search term.

Wireless technology

Desktop publishing developed at an astonishing speed. By the time I had acquired the numerous items that constituted a DTP system, I had also acquired a bundle of leads and cables that dangled from my desk.

So when I heard about wireless technology (I don't quite remember when that was) I was interested. I thought 'Whiffy' was an odd term for it until it was politely pointed out to me that it was actually pronounced 'WhyFye' and written as WiFi. It was not, happily, a technology that emitted the odour of a damp spaniel.

There are, of course, innumerable benefits that WiFi has brought us. It is still something of a surprise to me that it actually took quite so long to develop wireless systems for computing. After all, the radio wireless of the 20th century was a technological development that served the broadcasting and communication needs of its generation and indeed of subsequent generations since. Thankfully, we do have WiFi for computing now with perhaps the greatest benefit, with 4G and 5G, is access to the Internet on the move.

WiFi took a long time to settle down. With my first provider, Virgin, I had to pray to Mother Mary to make it work. One minute everything was fine and dandy, the next the connection faltered and crawled to a grinding halt. I would contact Virgin and kindly inform the call-handler that yes, my router is plugged in and switched on and yes I have already switched it off and on again – twice. I wonder again about what it is about switching things on and off. Does it give the fairies time to wave their fairy magic wands and put everything right? I was usually advised that it was a gremlin in the works (so not a fairy then) and that I could "try moving it around". This sounds like reasonable advice but the most reliable connection when 'moving it around' seemed to manifest only when the router was suspended in mid-air and at arm's length. This was not satisfactory. I would try lowering it gently to its nearest resting place but no, like returning a baby softly from an embrace to its cot, it protested. Although I am sure Virgin works for many, I have changed providers and WiFi now works all of the time. And that's because I have Zen.

Voice recognition

Towards the end of the 1990s, I had developed stiffness and aches in my hands, particularly in my fingers. There was a lot of talk then about Repetitive Strain Injury (RSI) which in the world of computing seemed to result from the excessive use of a keyboard. My work was now almost entirely computer-based, apart from attendance at a few meetings and the time I spent drawing freehand which wasn't very much. So that was it. I had RSI and I needed to do something about it. Perhaps I could talk to the computer (on the understanding that it wouldn't answer back). Perhaps it would do as I say without me having to use my hands. It did seem a good idea. After all, human communication is still best served through speech.

Of course, I was by no means the only computer operator to have thought about this. Several companies were springing up offering speech recognition software for just this reason. One of particular note claimed that it could learn the user's voice and the more the user spoke the greater the accuracy would be. This sounded just right. To get a head start in this respect I was encouraged by the software to dictate the story of Goldilocks and the Three Bears so it would indeed 'learn my voice'. This did raise the odd eyebrow. When a colleague knocked on the door and entered at the very moment I was asking why Goldilocks had eaten *my* porridge, all I could say by way of explanation was "I am Baby Bear."

"I'll come back later", she said. "I see you are busy."

I continued undeterred, if somewhat embarrassed. As soon as I had trained the software to detect the tones of my voice I was away. At least so I thought. I understood that it was going to take a bit of getting used to, not least because the technical terms commonly used throughout the water and sanitation sector were not, as far as I could tell, in the lexicon of Goldilocks, and certainly not that of the Three Bears.

No matter. I opened a new document and in the voice of my parents described earlier, I spoke unreasonably loudly at it to give it a title:

"The Warmer, Engine and Develop meant Census."

Now I do have a natural tendency to mumble so I was prepared to give the software a chance and with greater focus on my diction and increasing the volume of my voice yet further to that just short of a shout, after a few tries I came close to "The Water, Engineering and Development Centre".

I persisted for some time. The product suggested that it was 95 percent accurate and as I assumed it was still learning my voice it wouldn't be long before I got better results.

The software was American. In itself, that is not a surprise. It featured a number of commands to navigate around a document and correct errors, which was a neat feature, even though the phraseology came from America. I had a go at deleting the last line of the paragraph I had just spoken. With punishing timing, for a second time, my colleague returned to be greeted by a forceful and rather aggressive command to "go to bottom and scratch that." Such a comment could lead to a disciplinary hearing.

This time I explained what I was up to and that all I meant was that the software should delete the last line I had dictated from the page. All was forgiven. She wouldn't take it any further, but did suggest that it might be wise to post a note on my door any time I had the urge to talk to myself.

I continued now that I had been cleared of any wrong-doing. But I became more and more frustrated making a catalogue of errors which took too long to correct. The final straw came when I dictated a totally indecipherable line. Then out of nowhere, additional words appeared below the last scrambled line of the document:

"Oh, four foxes, ache".

I'd had enough. I decided to change my keyboard for one with a lighter touch and stocked up with Ibuprofen. As it turned out I didn't have RSI. It was something else, but that's a story for another time.

Speech recognition has improved immeasurably. It appears in several guises, not least in phone applications. You don't have to narrate a fairy tale before you use it, which is a boon, but it's still rare that I can dictate a message without having to make at least one or two manual corrections.

Changing Realities

Mobile phones

The story of the development of mobile phones is a curious one. From the size of a common brick, they became smaller and lighter. With market forces at play, they reduced in size to the point at which it was

Figure 15. Samsung phones shrunk to 100mm (right) but grew again when features beyond calling and texting were introduced and the phone became more than that just a phone. It became a 'smartphone' (left).

possible to sneak them into a pocket or a handbag. And then they got bigger again.

Initially, the smaller sized phone was appealing, as was the keypad which also now featured alphabetic characters and punctuation marks as well as numbers. Without really knowing it we had entered the era of text messaging – or as we now say – texting.

Texting became as much a function of mobile phones as talking was. The Short Message Service (SMS) emerged in a roundabout way from early digital information systems dating back to the 1970s and electrical telegraph systems dating back to the nineteenth century. So in some ways, texting wasn't really new. What *was* new, however, is that such systems were now engineered in miniature. So, in 1992, Neil Papworth, a 22-year-old test engineer for Sema Group in the UK, used a personal computer to send the text message 'Merry Christmas' to a mate via the Vodafone network.

This is a quaint story, but as is the way with 'Progress', nobody actually asked the populace whether or not we wanted our lives to become quite so dominated by text messaging. At least no one asked me. Considering my track record of forays into new technology, I would probably have replied: "nah, it's not for me".

And in a sense, it wasn't, at least at first. Texting was for younger people – people who (a) had the ability to relate an alphabetical character to a group of numerical ones by drumming numbers repeatedly at speed to select the right letter; and (b) could dislocate their thumbs so that a message could be composed as quickly as it could be spoken, if not quicker.

This was not my experience. I had problems with both. I am not generally a dim person, but I was when it came to this way of texting. It's not that it was just my hands that were dicky, it was my brain too. True, I was resistant to the idea of texting from the outset having a firm belief that I could just jolly well phone people up if I needed to contact them.

Nevertheless, I persevered to the extent that I could manage 'OK'. Masters of the art, my children, could rattle off messages ten to the dozen. If they ever wanted a lift I would text 'OK'. If I had to relay the time and location by text also, then to be honest, it would usually have been quicker for them to catch the bus. In part, this was because I like the English language in its current form. By this I mean I feel bound to relate messages in long hand. I could never bring myself to text 'C U in 10'. It would have to be 'I'll see you in about ten minutes', which by this time would be more like twenty.

I missed the Qwerty comfort blanket. Surely this had to be the way forward, even though I stuck to the principle that speaking was a more efficient and natural form of communication than typing. Eventually, you could pick a 'Blackberry'. (Why so many computer manufacturers like to call their products after fruit or nuts I've no idea... Acorn, Apple, Apricot, Blackberry. If it were me I'd dare to be different and turn to veg, but I suppose The Turnip might not sell as well.)

My first mobile phone was a Nokia and as soon as I could I leapfrogged to an iPhone 6 which featured the beloved Qwerty keypad. The advantages of texting were now obvious as I could now compose reasonably lucid messages with predictive text, although that too presented a challenge. Like dad dancing, I was dad texting.

Immediately though, I could see that there was a clear downside to text messaging which mirrored the downside of telephones in their early days. At home, in the 60s and 70s, I could be having an engaging conversation with the closest of friends about the Subbuteo team I would get next until the phone rang and all hell broke loose. Usually, one of my parents would shout: "It's the phone, pick up the phone will you, for goodness sake pick it up'". I did. "Who on earth is that now?" At this point my friend would leave telling me that they'd catch me later. Why we let the telephone trump live conversation is one of life's great mysteries.

And so it is with texting. You see it everywhere. Couples in cafés, both of them looking down at their phones; children ignoring parents; parents ignoring children. An incoming text bleeps in the middle of a conversation. "I'll just get that".

I try not to do this, but there are times when of course I do. There should be an additional item entered into the Lord's Prayer. "Forgive us our trespasses and all the times this week I have ignored people because I've been texting." This should be a commandment to follow, as the very beauty of messaging is that messages are stored for you to respond to as and when appropriate. To be fair, social pressures, particularly on younger people, run deep, and 'fomo' – the fear of missing out – is an uncomfortable feeling best avoided. I would like to think that more mindful social protocols will emerge to moderate our social interactions between technology and life, but I don't see any sign of them yet. Perhaps I never will.

Social media

This brings me neatly to social media in general. Foreseen long ago, it is now all around us. My memory of how we let it into our lives is a little sketchy. There was MSN, and Friends Reunited both trumped by Facebook, Twitter, Instagram, Linkedin, WhatsApp, TikTok and others I've missed and others that will surely come.

There is an upside to these many innovative ways of communicating with each other, of course, but there is a real downside too. We can be, and are, presented with false information – fake news. We can come across entrenched and uncompromising viewpoints from some people who have no consideration of where other people are at, or that there can be other ways of looking at life. It leads to fear, depression and even suicide. The dark web is *very* dark.

The silver lining to the iCloud is that these disparate means of information and communication can also shine a light on isolation, falsehood and oppression. We just have to make sure we keep the light shining so that reality doesn't become entirely virtual, augmented or artificial in ways that can harm our experience of being human.

Virtual and augmented realities

That's not to say that virtual reality isn't fun. As is the way I am, I scoffed at the very notion of virtual reality when I first heard about it. What's wrong with the real world? Can you feel the warmth of the spring sunshine, smell the sweet scent of a rose, embrace the spectacle of rolling hills and snow-topped mountains – virtually? Of course not! What You See Is Not What You Are Getting!

But therein lies the point. Although most of us will at some point in our lives have felt the warmth of the spring sunshine and smelt the sweet scent of a rose, there are many people who may not have had the opportunity to witness the beauty of rolling hills, much less that of snow-topped mountains. As for me, I had never known what it must have been like in Arles at the time of Vincent Van Gogh until I took a virtual trip back in time and space and saw it for myself in 3D. It was very cool.

As for augmented reality, I'm on dodgy ground as I don't know much about it. According to Wikipedia, 'Augmented reality (AR) is an interactive experience of a real-world environment where the objects that reside in the real world are enhanced by computer-generated perceptual information ... AR can be defined as a system that incorporates three basic features: a combination of real and virtual worlds, real-time interaction, and accurate 3D registration of virtual and real objects'[22].

So does that mean that computers could take over the world, an argument that seems to have sprung up in the press, perhaps out of fear of the future? I leave that question hanging for now and refer instead back to games of chess in 1996 and 1997 between an IBM computer, and Garry Kasparov, the then world chess champion.

The first series of matches were played in Philadelphia between an IBM computer system called 'Deep Thought' and Kasparov in 1996. Kasparov won by four games to two. It was curious that Deep Thought could win even one game so a rematch was played in New York City in 1997 and this time with an enhanced system renamed Deep Blue. The IBM so-called 'super-computer' won. Was this 'Game Over' for the human brain?

Well not quite, but it heralded a new relationship between humankind and the machine. As with every development of computer-based technology and systems, augmented reality can be used for good or ill. Our duty is to use it for good because it is here for good.

And so now is AI – Artificial Intelligence – and it is coming at a pace in very many guises.

E-commerce

For the time being, I return to more familiar territory: commerce. Not that I know a lot about commerce beyond selling the odd painting or print and maybe a few copies of this book, but I find that the way the Internet has so dramatically changed how business is conducted all rather interesting.

To recap. As i mentioned earlier, 'Business' was one of the early adopters of the Internet for doing, well, business. As a result, commerce flourished as consumers found that the convenience of having parcels landing on the doorstep was quite a good way of buying stuff for those of us in particular who don't see shopping as a raison d'être. It's not that I dislike shopping, it's a privilege after all to have the means to buy things we need, a privilege not extended to everyone. It's just that physically browsing a real shop is tiring as I'm not good at standing about but it's the mulling over, the decision-making that is much easier to do sitting down with a laptop and a cup of coffee. True it's easier to select the wrong number of items without noticing. Had I, on one occasion, gone to a real shop, I might have found that it was odd to be pushing six bags of bananas to the checkout.

For understandable reasons, in the early days and weeks of the COVID-19 pandemic, online shopping was the only way to shop because all other types of shops were shut. I understand that for some people this was genuinely devastating as going to the shops and meeting up with mates at the same time was an important staple of social life. For me though it didn't matter so much, except for the unsettling thought that online shopping is undeniably contributing to the steady decline of the vibrancy and heart of many towns and cities across the country. In the town I live in today, many units are closed and I find this a huge shame and wish it wasn't so.

The wider, even sinister aspect of shopping online is that the more I buy, the more data is collected about what I buy, when I buy it and from whom. This has of course been happening for years at supermarkets, but now it happens everywhere. The chilling reality is that the online algorithms that sift through and analyse a good deal of our personal data means that when it comes to shopping What *They* See Is What You Get.

The Future

Artificial Intelligence

So, what of the future? It is tempting to indulge in a few predictions here, but my track record of predicting anything relating to technology or indeed any other aspect of life is woeful. I never thought that the 2016 Brexit Referendum would amount to anything more than a mild attempt to appease the far right wing of the Conservative Party; that anyone would seriously entertain the idea that Boris Johnson would become Prime Minister; or that the American people would prefer Donald Trump as President over every other candidate, including Hilary Clinton and, as I write this maybe Kamala Harris too. So the best I can do is take a few flights of fancy about the future as far, that is, as it relates to tech.

However, of one thing I *am* sure, is that this isn't the end of the story. It isn't even the beginning of the end. Artificial Intelligence (AI) is here now and will be the dominant force in technology in the years to come. That's not me saying this. Bill Gates is saying it and countless others close to the development of AI are saying it too. They should know. Virtual Reality is old news. It's now all about AI which is no longer just a convenient two-letter word for a pale-throated sloth you use at the fag end of a game of Scrabble.

Clearly, the future of AI holds immense potential and is likely to have a significant impact on various aspects of our lives. I've been trying to get my head around it and there are a few points I've been mulling over regarding the future of AI, including its current benefits, potential benefits, the downside, our fears, and ethical issues. For the latter of these, you could do worse than listen to Radio 4's Moral Maze on AI aired in 2023[23], although by the time I actually get around to finishing this book, that too might be old news.

So what are the benefits of AI? I wasn't sure, so I asked ChatGPT and it had this to say.

Advantages of AI

1. *Automation:* AI has the capability to automate repetitive tasks, leading to increased efficiency and productivity in various industries.

2. *Personalization:* AI algorithms can analyse vast amounts of data to provide personalized recommendations and experiences to users, enhancing customer satisfaction.

3. *Medical advancements:* AI has the potential to revolutionize healthcare by aiding in early disease detection, improving diagnostics, and enabling more precise treatment plans.

4. *Enhanced safety:* AI-powered systems can improve safety measures in areas such as transportation, surveillance, and disaster management, reducing human errors and enhancing response times.

5. *Data analysis:* AI techniques enable organizations to extract valuable insights from large datasets, leading to better decision-making and strategic planning.

Other potential benefits of AI

1. *Scientific discoveries:* AI can assist in accelerating scientific research by processing vast amounts of data, identifying patterns, and generating hypotheses for further exploration.

2. *Improved education:* AI-based educational tools can provide personalized learning experiences, adapt to the needs of an individual student, and enhance access to quality education globally.

3. *Sustainable solutions:* AI can contribute to finding more sustainable solutions for energy management, resource allocation, and environmental monitoring, aiding in the fight against climate change.

4. *Assistance to the elderly and disabled:* AI-powered robots and assistive technologies can improve the quality of life for elderly individuals and people with disabilities by providing support in daily activities and healthcare monitoring.

So what's not to like? Bring it on. But before I got too carried away with AI, I did think I should ask ChatGPT what it had to say about it's disadvantages. Again, obligingly, it set them out for me.

Disadvantages of AI

1. *Job displacement:* The automation capabilities of AI may lead to job displacement in certain industries, necessitating workforce re-skilling and transition programmes.

2. *Bias and discrimination:* If not carefully developed and monitored, AI algorithms can perpetuate existing biases present in training data, leading to discriminatory outcomes.

3. *Privacy concerns:* The increasing use of AI technologies can raise concerns about data privacy and security, as personal information may be collected, analyzed, and potentially misused.

4. *Lack of human judgment:* AI systems lack human-level judgment and understanding, making them prone to errors and incapable of considering nuanced ethical or moral dilemmas.

5. *Dependency and reliability:* Over-reliance on AI systems without appropriate fail-safe mechanisms could lead to catastrophic consequences if the systems malfunction or are manipulated.

Catastrophic consequences? Oh, my word. Maybe we might not want to bring it on right now or quite so wholeheartedly, but do we have a choice? There is the issue too with super-intelligence – speculation about the development of highly advanced AI systems surpassing human intelligence raising concerns about the loss of control and the impact on human civilization. There are ethical issues too. The increasing autonomy and decision-making capabilities of AI systems also raise concerns about the ethical implications of their actions, such as autonomous vehicles making life-or-death decisions. Although I rather like the idea of setting the satnav and settling down to read the paper; perhaps having the occasional snooze, letting the vehicle take me to a destination of my choice, I do get this point.

And it doesn't end there. Perhaps the most concerning aspect is that the widespread deployment of AI technologies can exacerbate societal divisions, concentrating power in the hands of a few if not managed appropriately.

So, it's clearly important to note that while AI has significant potential for positive impact, addressing these disadvantages, fears, and ethical issues is crucial to ensure its responsible and beneficial development and deployment in the future.

All this said, in the meantime, it's worth having a play. ChatGPT was able to prepare presentation notes for me on how to design an academic poster in just under thirty seconds. This was most helpful. It also wrote the lyrics to a song about the love/hate relationship one can have with Marmite. This was to accompany a dear friend playing the twelve-bar blues one evening at home for our joyful entertainment. It goes thus:

Well, I woke up this morning, feelin' kinda strange,
Craving something special, to set my taste buds free from their chains,
I stumbled to the kitchen, not knowin' what to find,
And then I saw that jar of Marmite, oh, it sure looked fine!

(Chorus)
Oh, Marmite, my Marmite, you're the flavour of my soul,
Spread you on some toast, and you make my senses whole,
A savoury sensation, a taste that can't be beat,
Oh, Marmite, my Marmite, you make my life complete!

It goes on, but best I leave it there.

I have also ventured into AI for image generation initially using a program called 'Fotor'. This worked with less satisfying results. Some of the figures I asked it to sketch out were returned to my desktop with multiple contorted limbs, usually more than the standard four. Now Adobe has stepped in with 'Firefly', and to coin a phrase 'things can only get better'. All this is happening at an overwhelming rate. As I was playing around with Firefly, I uploaded one of my drawings (of a donkey carrying two jerrycans of water) and asked Firefly to create a similar image based on my style of ink drawing. The results weren't perfect as the Firefly version doesn't represent plastic jerrycans, but some other fictional type of container. But otherwise, it's done a good job – perhaps a better job as the graphic intensity and contrast of the donkey itself is maximized. This is leaving me with another existential crisis on my hands. Is my role as an illustrator now about describing a picture rather than getting my hands dirty and creating it myself?

Figure 16. *Left:* My line drawing of a donkey carrying two 20 litre jeryycans of water. Time taken: 90 minutes.
Right: Having uploaded the drawing to Adobe Firefly and asked it to generate an image from a typed description it supplied the image on the right. Time taken: 90 seconds.

The distant future

As for the distant future, who can tell? AI is becoming rapidly integrated into everyday life and on everyday devices. Apple Intelligence is due to be released for iPhones any day soon. Perhaps Artificial Intelligence will no longer be 'artificial' and, along with quantum computing, will develop the computer to be just like us. The energy AI requires is huge but if we can harness enough, we might just be able to send the Machine off to far away worlds and it will not only send back reams of baffling data, but it too will marvel at the magnificence and rather scary nature of the Universe.

But what of *What You See Is What You Get*? Well, it looks like it's now a question of *What AI Thinks You Want Is What You Get*.

We'd better be careful what we wish for.

References

1. Copeland, B. Jack, 2000. *The Modern History of Computing*. Stanford Encyclopedia of Philosophy. Metaphysics Research Lab, Stanford University.

2. Turing, A. M., 1936. *On Computable Numbers with an Application to the Entschiedungs Problem*.
   Available at: https://www.cs.virginia.edu/~robins/Turing_Paper_1936.pdf

3. Swade, Doron, 2022. *The History of Computing: A Very Short Introduction*. Oxford. Oxford University Press.

4. *American Heritage Dictionary of the English Language*. Fifth edition, 2018. Boston. Houghton Mifflin Harcourt.

4. *Desert Island Discs: Bill Gates*. 2016. BBC Radio 4.

6. *The Computer Programme: Episode 1: It's Happening Now*. 1982. BBC Two.

7. 'Printing Press', 2024. *History.com*.
   Available at: https://www.histoy.com/topics/inventions/printing-press

8. 'Spirit Duplicator', 2024. *Wikipedia*.
   Available at:https://en.wikipedia.org/wiki/Spirit_duplicator

9. 'Rubber Cement', 2024. *Wikipedia*.
   Available at: https://en.wikipedia.org/wiki/Rubber_cement

10. 'Liquid paper', 2024. *Wikipedia*.
    Available at: https://en.wikipedia.org/wiki/Liquid_Paper

11. 'Alan Sugar', 2024. *Wikipedia*.
    Available at: https://en.wikipedia.org/wiki/Alan_Sugar

12 *The Computer Literacy Project Archive, 1980-1989*, 2024. BBC. Available at: https://clp.bbcrewind.co.uk
13 'Amstrad', 2024. *Wikipedia*. Available at: https://en.wikipedia.org/wiki/Amstrad
14 Dot matrix printing', 2024. *Wikipedia*. Available at: https://en.wikipedia.org/wiki/Dot_matrix_printing
15 ISO: Global standards for trusted goods and services, 2024. *ISO 32000-1:2008: Document management: Portable document format Part 1: PDF 1.7.* Available at: https://www.iso.org/standard/51502.html
16 'Typography' 2024. *Wikipedia*. Available at: https://en.wikipedia.org/wiki/Typography
17 Eno's Windows 95 start-up-up jingle: https://www.youtube.com/watch?v=I3Ak5VgyEoc
18 Eno's Windows 95 start-up-up jingle –slowed down to last an hour: https://www.youtube.com/watch?v=LSMW55-KfuY
19 Garfield, S., 2011. *Just My Type: A book about fonts.* London: Profile Books.
20 'Intel 80286,' 2024. *Wikipedia*. Available at: https://en.wikipedia.org/wiki/Intel_80286
21 'Vannevar Bush' 2024. *Wikipedia*. Available at: https://en.wikipedia.org/wiki/Vannevar_Bush
22 'Augmented reality' 2024. *Wikipedia*. Available at: https://en.wikipedia.org/wiki/Augmented_reality
23 *The Moral Maze: AI.* 2013. BBC Radio 4.

ROD SHAW
ART & DESIGN

www.rod-shaw.co.uk